KONTINENT

Alexander Solzhenitsyn
Andrei Sakharov
Andrei Sinyavsky
Joseph Brodsky
Alexander Galich
Igor Golomshtok
Vladimir Maramzin
Vladimir Maximov
Alexander Piatigorsky
Carl-Gustav Ströhm
Eugène Ionesco

*Editors of the first two volumes
of the Russian language edition*

Editor in chief **Vladimir Maximov**
Editorial secretary **Igor Golomshtok**

Editorial board
Raymond Aron, George Bailey,
Alexander Galich, Jerzy Giedroyc,
Gustaw Gerling-Grudzinski, Milovan
Djilas, Wolf Siedler, Eugène Ionesco,
Robert Conquest, Naum Korzhavin,
Victor Nekrasov, Ludek Pachman,
Andrei Sakharov, Ignazio Silone,
Andrei Sinyavsky, Archbishop Joann
of San Francisco, Yozef Chapski,
Zinaida Schakhovskoy, Alexander
Shmeman, Carl-Gustav Ströhm.

*Editorial advisers for the
English language edition*
Nicholas Bethell and Barry Rubin

PUBLISHER'S NOTE

Except for the articles by Andrei
Sakharov and Vladimir Maximov, the
contents of this edition have been
selected from Volumes I & II of the
original Russian language edition.

The explanatory notes which appear
both in square brackets and at the foot
of the page have been provided by the
translators and editors for the English
edition. Footnotes written by the
authors which appeared in the Russian
edition are described as such.

Kontinent

The Alternative Voice Of Russia And Eastern Europe

CORONET BOOKS
Hodder and Stoughton

Coronet Edition 1977

Printed in Great Britain for
Hodder and Stoughton Paperbacks,
a division of Hodder and Stoughton Ltd.,
Mill Road, Dunton Green, Sevenoaks, Kent
by Richard Clay (The Chaucer Press), Ltd.,
Bungay, Suffolk

ISBN 0 340 21317 5

Contents

CONTENTS

Statement from the Editors*

The birth of a new magazine is at once an occasion of joy and anguish; joy, because it opens up new vistas, inspires new hopes, and creates a new social and historical situation; and anguish, on account of the many doubts that arise in the process of designing its ideological content and literary form, and also on account of the disquieting apprehensions about the struggle that lies ahead, and the sublime responsibility which the founders of such a publication assume.

On occasions like this a parallel is usually drawn with Alexander Herzen's periodical *The Bell*. Unfortunately, under present conditions such a comparison can hardly be just. Herzen's journal was a strictly political publication, and not literary, for the simple reason that in the 'dark times of reactionary tsarism' one of man's finest literatures was born in Russia and developed without hindrance. In that time of 'slavery' no one, starting with Pushkin and Gogol and ending with Tolstoy and Dostoevsky, ever had to look for a publisher abroad. All native Russian writers worthy of any notice whatsoever, and we emphasise all, were published in their own country.

For the first time in history a situation has arisen when in all the countries of 'victorious socialism' from China to Cuba, where at last 'liberty, equality, and fraternity' have triumphed, any imaginative literature that comes into conflict with the ideological directives of the ruling apparatus is prosecuted as a criminal offence. A book thus becomes a piece of evidence, a proof of guilt, a crime, and a cause for punishment. Because of

* This statement, and the 'Words of Welcome' on pp. 11–14, are taken from the introductory material in the first Russian issue.

a book someone is exiled, as Joseph Brodsky was; because of a book someone is left to rot for years in a labour camp, as Andrei Sinyavsky was; because of a book someone is locked up in a lunatic asylum, as was Mikhail Naritsa. Not a single one of the dictatorships currently existing in the West can boast of ever having physically destroyed, hounded to death, driven to insanity and destitution, and exiled as many of its most brilliant literary figures, including two Nobel laureates, as we can count in the martyrologies of the countries with the most 'revolutionary' and 'progressive' social system.

It is for this reason that we consider it the task of our journal not only to engage in political polemics with militant totalitarianism, but above all to confront it with the combined creative force of Eastern European literature and spiritual thought, which have been enriched by the most bitter personal experience and by the resulting perception of a new historical prospect.

What are the aims and principles of our journal? What is its moving spirit? And what is it guided by in its everyday functions? Here is how we formulate these principles for ourselves:

1. ABSOLUTE RELIGIOUS IDEALISM, that is, with a given dominant Christian tendency, a constant spiritual union with representatives of other faiths.

2. ABSOLUTE ANTI-TOTALITARIANISM, that is, a struggle against any variety of totalitarianism – Marxist, nationalist or religious.

3. ABSOLUTE DEMOCRATISM, that is, consistent support of all democratic institutions and tendencies in contemporary society.

4. ABSOLUTE NON-PARTISANSHIP, that is, a categorical refusal to express the interests of any existing political group.

We feel that these four articles of faith can become a sufficiently broad but at the same time principled basis for the unification and collaboration of all anti-totalitarian forces in Eastern Europe in their dialogue with the West.

The question naturally arises: why the name *Kontinent*? We were attracted mainly by the range of its meaning. We speak on behalf of a whole continent of East European culture.

Behind us stretches a huge continent dominated by **totalitari-anism**, with a boundless archipelago of cruelty and violence extending over its entire length. And, finally, we are striving to create around us a united continent of all the forces of anti-totalitarianism in the spiritual struggle for the freedom and dignity of Man. Moreover, we – Eastern and Western Europe – are the two halves of the same continent, and we must hear and understand each other before it is too late.

He that hath ears to hear, let him hear!

Some Words of Welcome

The appearance of a new journal, *Kontinent*, also stirs new hopes. For the first time since attempts in the USSR to publish *samizdat* journals in no way subservient or conforming to the official ideology were nipped in the bud, and since the only honest and serious journal, *Novy mir*, was ravaged, the Russian intelligentsia is attempting to unite its thoughts and works without regard for either the will of officials or its own division by political boundaries. This is neither the ideal form nor ideal territory for the publication of a free Russian journal; how much more joyous our hearts would be if all the authors and the publisher were located on native Russian soil. But under present-day conditions this is clearly not possible.

However, the plan of the journal reveals to us a new side of its task: *for a start*, it will be published in Russian and German and we may clearly expect editions in other European languages. And so our straitened and scattered condition is turning into a new hope: the journal would like to become international, to combine the efforts of not just Russian writers and concentrate the attention of not just Russians. Today, when all the dangers and tasks of society cannot be contained within national boundaries, such a turn is natural and fruitful.

If we read the proposal even more carefully, we see that it contains names that are highly esteemed and widely known in Eastern Europe; so that, considering the array of honorary members and the make-up of the editorial committee, we can expect a preponderance of voices and opinions from that part of the world. From this we can see an even more interesting prospect for the journal: it may become a genuine voice of Eastern Europe aimed at those Western ears which have not been blocked off from the truth and want to hear it. Only forty years ago, it would have been inconceivable that Russian, Polish, Hungarian, Czech, Rumanian, German, and Lithuanian writers might have a similar life experience, draw similar bitter conclusions from it, and have almost identical desires for the future. Today, this miracle, for which we have had to pay so dearly, has come to pass. The intelligentsia of Eastern Europe speaks in a single voice of suffering and knowledge. May great honour come to *Kontinent* if it can express this voice effectively. Woe to Western Europe (and very soon) if its ear remains indifferent.

Wishes often exceed what later actually happens. May it turn out differently this time.

ALEXANDER SOLZHENITSYN
June 1974

* * *

Dear Maximov,

I bid you welcome. It is a great honour for me to be among your contributors, alongside the great Solzhenitsyn and others.

Indeed, the problem is to find new bases on which to build a society that is less unacceptable than those that have been constructed up to now. We are well aware that the society of profit is condemnable and condemned. We know that societies called 'socialist' are worse than societies called 'liberal': in the name of justice and freedom power has been assumed by tyranny, corruption, arbitrary rule, injustice, censorship, and crime.

This is beginning to be realised. But the intellectuals of Western countries, at least many of them, do not want to acknowledge it. In France one segment of the intellectuals is 'left'. The other segment is 'right' or centrist. This means that the country is virtually in a state of civil war. We are at the mercy of economic crisis and everything may topple. Meanwhile, the 'left' bourgeois hate the 'right' bourgeois so much that they would like to put an end to them. Afterwards, anything can happen – it is none of their concern: dictatorship, prisons, repression, the suffocation of all freedoms, and even, so much the worse, collective annihilation. In reality, it is clear that every person hates his own self in others. Evidently, man is not very attractive morally nowadays, and in order not to hate ourselves, we must make a great effort at transcendence and courage.

What we lack is a new doctrine, left and non-Marxist (as was envisaged by Emmanuel Mounier and Denis de Rougemont and is still desired by the editors of the review *Esprit* grouped around Jean-Marie Domenach). This religion could be based on love or friendship. Eros, not Thanatos. I have had to overcome self-censorship to write the word 'love'. To speak of love and friendship in France, as well as religion and humanism, means to invite ridicule, to be laughed at. It is true that these words have been so besmirched that no one any longer knows what they are or what they mean, or else the 'hypocrite' who utters them is denounced.

If it is not 'love' that is spoken of in our day, then it is 'justice'. In actual fact, what people understand this word to mean is not equity but penalty, punishment, forced labour, the guillotine. As soon as a revolution comes to power, from 1789 until Stalin, with it come the tribunals.

What can we do if everything has failed? We don't care much for ourselves. To love another as we love ourselves means to hate him. Is a reversal still possible when we feel so close to apocalyptic catastrophe? It is Solzhenitsyn, Bukovsky, Amalrik, and yourself, and the hundreds of thousands of heroes, martyrs, saints perhaps, who perish in Bolshevik prisons – it is you and they who can still do something for this world.

As for the rest of us – I have in mind those of us who are open to your message – who have lived in freedom and ease while you were continually dying and coming back to life, only to die again, we have neither your experience nor your authority. Who knows, had we been in your shoes, whether or not we would have yielded to fear and pain, and the temptation to live in comfort and safety in your country, which so handsomely pays people who are ready to serve the régime.

It is you who should enlighten us, only you can still do this.

EUGÈNE IONESCO
July 1974

*   *   *

The creation of a new journal of literature and public opinion seems to me very necessary and timely. Its task now is to provide a maximum of factual information about the socialist countries and about the entire world.

I expect the literary section of *Kontinent* to shed light on the more profound aspects of life which are accessible to an intuitive perception of art. I am certain that the journal will make its contribution to the extremely important process, common to all mankind, of forming and reconstructing the philosophical, moral, and ethical values so lacking in contemporary humanity, which is preoccupied with the present day and is disillusioned.

I hope that all sections of this new publication will be interesting, talented, diverse in genre and subject matter, and will bring the reader not only knowledge, but spontaneous joy as well.

Kontinent has one particular feature that I should like to say a few words about. Its contributors are people who have spent a significant part of their lives in socialist countries. The reality of these countries is an historical phenomenon very poorly understood in the West. Its social, economic, and spiritual characteristics cannot be comprehended from the window of a tourist bus or from the official socialist press. Therefore, these people have something to tell the world and it would be hard to overestimate this opportunity.

I hope this new journal, born in difficult conditions, will find its readers and be of help to people and liked by them.

Unfortunately, I can merely dream that this journal will be available not only in the West, but to many people in the East, too. All the same, let us hope!

ANDREI SAKHAROV
Moscow, September 1974

The Solzhenitsyn / Sakharov Controversy

Foreword by **Vladimir Maximov**

On Alexander Solzhenitsyn's
A Letter to the Soviet Leaders
Andrei Sakharov

Sakharov and the Criticism of
A Letter to the Soviet Leaders
Alexander Solzhenitsyn

Foreword

VLADIMIR MAXIMOV

Many people, applying historical criteria to this (I think) most instructive controversy, have drawn a parallel with the battle between the Slavophiles and the Westernisers which exercised Russian minds in the second half of the nineteenth century.

But in this case (as, I believe, in every other) the historical approach to modern phenomena does no more than simplify the problem. It does not solve it. History can show close similarities between numerous events and situations, but it does not repeat itself. If it did, life, instead of being a line of ascent, would be a recurring cycle, closed in upon itself and quite banal.

In this dialogue between Solzhenitsyn and Sakharov – I emphasise that it is a dialogue, not an argument – there is a total absence of that element of irreconcilability, bitterness and anger that have accompanied the verbal battles of other inexperienced democrats and old-fashioned patriots. Quite simply, two great thinkers of modern Russia are examining, calmly and in depth, each in his own way, the problem of their people's and their country's future.

The conversation began with Alexander Solzhenitsyn's now famous *Letter to the Soviet Leaders*, in which the writer perceives the root of the evil of modern Russia to lie entirely in the *ideology* which rules there. He sees that Russia can be cleansed only through rejecting this ideology and then through universal repentance.

In this *Letter* Solzhenitsyn has even avoided his customary sharp polemical tone. Instead we detect an appeal, a warning, as well as his pain and grief for his native land, ground down by an ideology foreign to its spirit. But there is no polemicism.

Sakharov's reply came quickly, but in this reply there is not the slightest hint of any desire to join battle. The last thing he wants to do is to cross swords. In a tone which shows his great respect for his opponent, his companion-in-arms during many years of struggle against the same ideology, a great scientist uses scrupulous analytical argument to point out to a great writer the basic mistake in his version of today's and tomorrow's Russia. Ideology is not the most important evil, he says, ideology is merely a convenient façade for those in power.

The rest is to be found in the actual text of Alexander Solzhenitsyn's reply.

June 1975

On Alexander Solzhenitsyn's
'A Letter to the Soviet Leaders'

ANDREI SAKHAROV

Solzhenitsyn sent his letter to the Soviet leaders on 5 September 1973. Soon after his exile from the Soviet Union it was published abroad* and read in extracts over the radio. It is a statement by an author of unchallengeable international reputation, carefully thought out and expressing an essential part of his views on major political issues; I therefore consider it most important that it should be seriously debated, especially by the representatives of independent political thought in our country. For my own part, I am particularly conscious of the need to react publicly to Solzhenitsyn's letter, in that it has much in common with (and also makes veiled criticisms of) certain of my former political statements, most of which I would still stand by, even though I have reconsidered some of them. Above all, however, I am motivated by my disagreement with certain fundamental tenets of Solzhenitsyn's letter.

There is no question that Solzhenitsyn is one of the outstanding writers and political commentators of our time. The individual style, dramatic conflicts and vivid images in his works reflect positions on major political, moral and philosophical problems which the author has forged for himself in adversity. Solzhenitsyn's special and unique contribution to the spiritual history of our country lies in his accurate and uncompromising revelation of ordinary people's sufferings, and of the régime's crimes, unprecedented in their secrecy and their undiscriminating cruelty. This contribution of Solzhenitsyn's

---

* Solzhenitsyn's letter was first published in Russian by the YMCA Press in Paris. An English translation by Hilary Sternberg appeared in the *Sunday Times* on 3 March 1974 and was published by Wm Collins and Sons.

was made manifest in his *One Day in the Life of Ivan Denisovich* and now in his great work *The Gulag Archipelago*, before which I can only bow my head. Whatever one may think of Solzhenitsyn's attitude to this or that problem, one cannot over-value his creative writing – and he is far from having said yet all that he wants to say. In his letter Solzhenitsyn speaks again of the sufferings and sacrifices which have befallen our people in the last sixty years. He writes with particular conviction and distress about the lot of women, who are often forced to make up the family budget by combining housework and the up-bringing of children with tedious paid work in a way which has led to a deterioration in child-rearing and imposed a great strain on family life. He writes with similar persuasiveness about the widespread drunkenness, which has reached the proportions of a national scourge, about the pilfering, squandering and avoidance of work practised by all state employees, and about the ravaging of our towns, villages, rivers, forests and soils. Like Solzhenitsyn, I consider the achievements our propaganda system likes to boast of negligible beside the effects of over-strain, disillusionment and depression, and the consequent impairment of human relations and degradation of the human spirit.

However, even this critical and expository section of the letter reveals certain peculiarities in the author's approach which make me uneasy and disappointed, feelings which mount on reading further. It is, for example, very conspicuous that Solzhenitsyn singles out especially the sufferings and sacrifices of the *Russian* people. Now, of course, anyone has a perfect right to write and be concerned about what he knows best, what touches him most nearly and personally, but we all know that the horrors of the civil war, the de-kulakisation,* the famine, the terror, the Second World War, the historically unprecedented harsh and tyrannical repression exercised against millions of those returning from captivity, the persecution of believers, we know that all these horrors fell in absolutely equal measure upon Russian and non-Russian subjects of the Soviet empire alike. Indeed certain measures, such as forced

---

* The expropriation of land from kulaks, i.e. the better-off peasants, and in practice also those peasants who resisted the State's policy of forced collectivisation of agriculture.

deportation, genocide, the struggle against national liberation movements and the repression of national cultures, were actually for the most part the privilege of the non-Russians. Today, moreover, we learn that the schoolchildren of Uzbekistan, whose progress is vaunted to foreign visitors, have to spend many months each year in the cotton plantations instead of at their lessons, and are nearly all ill from breathing in weed-killers. I feel that, in discussing questions of the magnitude of those raised by Solzhenitsyn, all this cannot just be ignored. Nor must one forget that each nation in our country bears its share in our historic guilt as well as in such constructive work as has been accomplished, and that, whatever any individual may wish, their fates are bound to remain indissolubly linked for a long time to come.

Solzhenitsyn proclaims that the chief dangers facing our country are war with China and the pollution of the environment, along with the exhaustion of natural resources caused by excessive industrialisation and urbanisation. Both these dangers he considers to have been generated by blind adherence to ideas from the West: the dogma of unlimited scientific and technical progress, which he more or less equates with the unlimited quantitative growth of large-scale industrial production, and especially Marxist dogma, which in his view is a manifestation of the soulless anti-religious nature of Western culture. Solzhenitsyn states that it was Marxist dogma that was responsible for the economic absurdity of the collective farms, which brought about the tragedy of the peasantry in the 1930s and which underlies the economic difficulties of the country to the present day. That dogma has led to the bureaucratisation of the economy and to those extremes which force us today to hawk the country's natural riches around the world. That same dogma requires us to pay Latin American revolutionaries, Arab nationalists and Vietnamese guerrillas out of the people's pockets and forces us to threaten the world with nuclear weapons, thereby endangering and bankrupting not only other nations, but ourselves as well. That same dogma embroils us with China more dangerously than any territorial disputes and at the same time deprives us of weapons against her.

I have outlined Solzhenitsyn's arguments here rather freely, in my own way, as I understand them. Many of his thoughts seem to me both significant and apt, and I welcome this new and talented defence of them. Nevertheless, I must state that in certain very important respects Solzhenitsyn's arguments strike me as misguided, precisely where they touch on the least trivial issues. I will begin with a question which is perhaps less significant in terms of its immediate effects, but is nevertheless very important in principle. Solzhenitsyn very aptly describes various anomalies and costly absurdities in our internal affairs and our foreign policy, and he does so with justified indignation and compassion for his countrymen. But his view of them as directly generated by ideological causes seems to me somewhat schematic. I see present-day Soviet society as being marked rather by ideological indifference and the cynical use of ideology as a convenient façade: expediency and flexibility in the manipulation of slogans goes along with traditional intolerance towards free-thinking 'from below'. Stalin committed his crimes not from ideological motives but as part of the struggle for power, while he was building a new 'barrack-square' type of society (as Marx called it); in the same way, the present leaders' main criterion, when facing any difficult decisions, is the conservation of their own power and of the basic features of the system.

I also find it difficult to accept Solzhenitsyn's view of Marxism as a 'Western' and anti-religious doctrine which distorted a healthy Russian line of development. The very classification of ideas as Western or Russian is incomprehensible to me. In my view, a scientific and rational approach to social and natural phenomena is only compatible with a classification of ideas and concepts as true or false. And where are we to discern this healthy Russian line of development? Has there ever been a time in the history of Russia, or any other nation, when development was possible without contradictions and upheavals?

What Solzhenitsyn says about ideological rituals and the intolerable waste of the time and energy of millions of people on drivel which only accustoms them to fatuity and hypocrisy – all this is undoubtedly true and makes a strong impression, but the point is that in our situation this hypocritical drivel is taking the place of an 'oath of allegiance': it binds people by mutual responsibility for the shared sin of hypocrisy. It is simply a further example of an expedient absurdity generated by the system.

I find Solzhenitsyn's treatment of the problem of progress particularly misleading. Progress is a world-wide process, which must not be equated, certainly not in the times to come, with the quantitative growth of large-scale industrial production. Given universal scientific and democratic control of the economy and of the whole of social life, including population growth, this, I am quite convinced, is not a utopia but a vital necessity. Progress must continually change its immediate forms according to need, in order to meet the requirements of human society while preserving at all costs the natural environment and the earth for our descendants. To slow down scientific research, international scientific contacts, technological experiment and the introduction of new agricultural systems can only delay the solution of these problems and create critical situations for the whole of humanity.

Solzhenitsyn's most dramatic assertion concerns the problem of China. He feels that our country is threatened, owing to the struggle for ideological supremacy, and also to demographic pressure, by imminent total war with China over the Asiatic territories of the USSR. He predicts that that war will be the most protracted and costly in human history, and that there will be no victors, only general devastation and a return to savagery. Solzhenitsyn urges meeting that threat by renouncing ideological rivalry, awakening Russian patriotism, and developing the north-east of the country. Some time ago I expressed similar fears in my 'Memorandum'. I now think that this view over-dramatises a situation which is, of course, by no means simple or devoid of dangers. The majority of China experts, I would say, are of the opinion that for quite a long time to come China will not have the military resources for a large-scale aggressive war against the USSR. It is hard to imagine that adventurers might emerge and drive the country to such a suicidal step. On the other hand, any Soviet aggression would also be doomed to failure. It may even be conjectured that exaggerating the Chinese threat is a political ploy of the Soviet leadership. In any case, overestimating the Chinese threat is a disservice to the cause of the democratisation and demilitarisation of our country, which we and the whole world so badly need. It goes without saying that the fate of the Chinese people, like that of many others in our world, is tragic and should be an object of concern to all men, including the United Nations. But that is a separate matter. In this problem of the conflict with China, which in my view is a geopolitical struggle for hegemony, Solzhenitsyn, as in other parts of his letter, over-estimates the role of ideology. In actual fact, the Chinese leaders seem to be just as pragmatic as the Soviet ones.

I will now proceed to an analysis of Solzhenitsyn's positive programme, aimed, as he says, at preventing war with China and stopping the destruction of Russia's natural life, land, and people. I will sum up his proposals in the following points; once again, of course, I am responsible for the wording, the order of propositions, and so on.

1. The withdrawal of state support for Marxism as the official and compulsory ideology ('separation of Marxism from the state').

2. The withdrawal of support for revolutionaries, nationalists and partisans all over the world, and the concentration of effort on internal problems.

3. The cessation of guardianship over Eastern Europe, and the release of the national republics from forced incorporation in the USSR.

4. An agrarian reform on the Polish model (my own wording).

5. The development of the north-east of the country not by innovative technology but by means already available, not by huge factories but by preserving the environment, the soil, peace and quiet, etc. What is envisaged seems to be the settlement of the north-east by communes of enthusiastic volunteers. Solzhenitsyn seems to me to regard these people as patriots inspired by national and religious aspirations. It is to them that he assigns the state's newly freed resources, the results of scientific research, and the opportunity to earn high personal income; in return they will create an advance guard against China, a conservatory (or 'settling tank', as he himself puts it) for the Russian nation, and a fundamental reservoir of wealth for the whole country.

6. An end to the selling off of national resources, natural gas, timber, etc.; economic isolationism as a corollary of military, political and ideological isolationism.

7. Disarmament, as far as the Chinese threat allows.

8. Democratic freedoms, toleration, the release of political prisoners.

9. The strengthening of the family and child-rearing; freedom of religious education.

10. The preservation of the party, while increasing the part played by the Soviets;* the preservation of the basic authoritarian features of the system is seen as permissible, provided the rule of law is assured and freedom of conscience guaranteed.

There is no doubt that Solzhenitsyn's programme is the fruit of serious reflection, and is the expression of a set of opinions which he holds with deep conviction. All the same, I am bound to say that it fills me with serious misgivings. One cannot but concur with the proposals contained in points 2, 3 and 4, though I should point out that in my outline I unintentionally heightened the priority given to point 3, which I consider paramount from the political and moral viewpoint: Solzhenitsyn himself mentions it only in a footnote. Point 1, which demands the abolition of official state protection for Marxism, is incontestable, but, as I say, I do not think one should overestimate the role of the ideological factor in present-day Soviet society.

Points 7, 8 and 9 are also incontestable, even though this is not the first time they have appeared in documents of the democratic movement. Their reiteration by an authoritative figure is welcome, and they are well argued in the letter.

In support of point 10 of his programme, Solzhenitsyn argues that our country may not yet be ready for a democratic system, and that an authoritarian system combined with legality and Orthodoxy cannot be as bad as all that if Russia managed to conserve its national vitality under such a system right into the twentieth century. These assertions of Solzhenitsyn's are alien to my way of thinking. I consider a democratic mode of development the only satisfactory one for any country. The centuries-old abject and servile Russian spirit, combined with suspicion of foreigners, seems to me a tremendous affliction, and not a sign of national vitality. Only democratic institutions

* The Soviets were the workers' and peasants' representative councils, in whose name the Bolsheviks seized power, and through which they exercised what very soon became in practice their own party's dictatorship.

can mature the national character so that it is capable of leading a sensible way of life in our ever more complicated world. Of course, this is a vicious circle which cannot be summarily broken, but I can see no reason why in our country it should be considered an impossible step. In Russia's past there have been a number of fine democratic achievements, starting with the reforms of Alexander II, which lead me to reject the arguments of people in the West who consider the failure of socialism in Russia to be the result of the country's peculiarities and the absence of democratic traditions.

The central points in Solzhenitsyn's programme are 5 and 6, and these require more detailed analysis. In the first place, I object to the notion that our country should be sealed off from the supposedly corrupting influence of the West, from trade and from what is known as 'the exchange of people and ideas'. The only form of isolationism which makes sense is for us to refrain from imposing our socialist messianism on other countries, to give up both secret and open support for subversion on other continents, and to cease the export of lethal weapons.

Can the extensive northern territories, with their severe climate, be opened up for intensive high-productivity cultivation in the present conditions of under-population and bad communications, just by using the economic and technical resources of our country, when its reserves are already strained to the utmost and are likely to remain so for a long time to come? I feel quite sure this is not possible. For that reason, to refuse international co-operation with the USA, West Germany, Japan, France, Italy, Britain, India, China and other countries, to bar the import of equipment, capital, technical ideas, and the immigration of workers would be to delay the assimilation of those territories in a way which would be intolerably selfish in view of the problems that face humanity as a whole. (It would be a dog-in-the-manger policy.) Furthermore, I am quite convinced, unlike Solzhenitsyn, that there is no really important problem in the world today which can be solved at the national level. Disarmament, in particular, so essential in order to eliminate the danger of war, can obviously only be undertaken in conjunction by all the major powers, on the basis of treaty obligations and trust. The same is true of birth control and the limitation of industrial growth, and of the transition to a technology harmless to the environment, which will inevitably be more expensive than our present technology. The solution of all these problems is frustrated by national egoism and rivalry between states.

A global approach is also necessary for the successful completion of the fundamental scientific and technical tasks facing us today, such as the creation of nuclear and thermonuclear systems of energy, the elaboration of new agricultural techniques, the production of synthetic substitutes for protein, the problem of urban construction, the development of an industrial technology harmless to the environment, the conquest of space, the struggle against cancer and cardio-vascular diseases, the elaboration of cybernetic techniques, and so on. These projects require huge expenditure, beyond the capacity of any single state.

In short, then, a strategy for the development of human society on earth, if it is to be compatible with the continuation of the human species, can only be worked out and put into practice on a global scale.

Our country cannot live in economic, scientific and technical isolation, without world trade – and that includes trade in the natural resources of our country – and cut off from the scientific and technical progress of the rest of the world, for the latter represents not only a danger, but also the only real chance to save humanity. Rapprochement with the West should constitute the first stage in a process of convergence (contrary to Solzhenitsyn's view) and should be accompanied by serious democratic reforms in the USSR, partly voluntary and partly induced by economic and political pressure from abroad. In particular, it is essential to reach a democratic solution to the problem of freedom of emigration from the USSR, as well as freedom to return, which affects Russians, Germans, Jews, Ukrainians, Lithuanians, Turks, Armenians and others, since this would render the retention of other anti-democratic institutions in the country impossible, it would become necessary to raise living standards closer to those obtaining in the West, and the free exchange of people and ideas would become possible.

More complicated is the question of de-centralising industry and organising it communally. It is my view that Solzhenitsyn and political commentators close to him much overestimate industrial gigantism as a cause of our contemporary problems. Optimal industrial structure depends on so many specific factors, technical, social, demographic, even climatic, that it would be absurd to lay down any universal standards. Moreover, the commune does not seem to me a panacea from all ills, though I do not deny its attractiveness in certain circumstances. Solzhenitsyn's dream of making do with the simplest technology, indeed virtually with manual labour, has an unpractical air at best, and in the harsh conditions of the north-east would be condemned in advance to failure. Solzhenitsyn's programme is mythmaking rather than practical politics, and myths are not always harmless especially in our twentieth-century world, which craves them. The myth of the 'settling tank' for the Russian nation could end in tragedy.

To sum up briefly some of my objections to Solzhenitsyn's letter: in my view Solzhenitsyn overestimates the role of the ideological factor in present-day Soviet society; hence his belief that the Russian people can be saved through the replacement of Marxism by a healthy ideology, which he apparently considers Orthodoxy to be. This conviction underlies his whole programme. But I am convinced that in reality the nationalist and isolationist tendencies of Solzhenitsyn's thought, and his own patriarchal religious romanticism, lead him into very serious errors and render his proposals utopian and even potentially dangerous.

Solzhenitsyn addresses his letter to the country's leaders, not just rhetorically, but in the genuine expectation of meeting with at least partial understanding among them. It is difficult to quarrel with such a desire. But is there anything in his proposals which is both new and acceptable to the country's leaders? Great Russian nationalism and the enthusiastic onslaught on virgin lands – these are programmes which have been tried before and are still being tried now. The appeal to patriotism is straight out of the arsenal of semi-official propaganda. One cannot help associating it with the notorious patriotic-militarist educational system and with the 'anti-cosmopolitan' campaign of the recent past. Stalin, during the war and up to his death, gave free rein to 'tamed' Orthodoxy. All these parallels with Solzhenitsyn's proposals should not only be apparent to us, but also make us wary.

It may be said that Solzhenitsyn's nationalism is not aggressive, but mild and defensive in character, only aiming to save and revive one of the most long-suffering of nations. History shows, however, that 'ideologists' are always milder than the practical politicians who follow in their footsteps. Amongst the Russian people and the country's leaders are a good many who sympathise with Great Russian nationalism, who are afraid of democratic reforms and of becoming dependent on the West. If they fall on such well-prepared soil, Solzhenitsyn's misconceptions could become dangerous.

I have felt it necessary to publish this statement mainly because of my disagreement with many of Solzhenitsyn's basic assertions. On the other hand I should like to emphasise again that, as a whole, the publication of Solzhenitsyn's letter is an important political event, another major contribution to the free discussion of key problems.

Even though some aspects of his outlook seem to me mistaken, nevertheless Solzhenitsyn is a tower of strength in the struggle for human dignity in our tragic world.

April 1974

Sakharov and the Criticism of 'A Letter to the Soviet Leaders'

ALEXANDER SOLZHENITSYN

All during 1974, as I awaited the publication of the collection of articles *From Under the Rubble*,* I refrained from replying to the abundant criticism of my *Letter to the Soviet Leaders*. The very fact the the *Letter* was addressed to whom it was did not allow me to provide a deep enough basis for my proposals. Now, however, that foundation will be revealed more clearly in my articles in *From Under the Rubble*. The criticism that has come from the intelligentsia of Moscow was astonishing not in and of itself, but mainly, I dare say, on account of its cold disregard of another document that was published *at the same time* and addressed directly to the Soviet intelligentsia: my essay 'Live Not by Lies'. Whether or not I ought to have addressed the Soviet rulers, whether my proposals to them were 'proper' or 'improper', and whether they abandon their ideology or not – none of this was of ultimate and sole importance, because a second and surer path was proposed – for *us* to follow. If *we* were to break with that ideology, and if *we* were to stop supporting that vicious scarecrow, it would collapse, the will of the 'leaders' notwithstanding. It is strange that this appeal, aimed directly at *us*, was *not noticed* by the verbose Moscow critics of my *Letter*. As the proverb says: Where things are simple angels abound, but where they are tricky there's not one around.

Western criticism was surprising for a different reason: its failure to read the *Letter* carefully. Beginning with hasty and irresponsible newspaper headlines, critics reacted as though

* This collection first appeared in Moscow (under the title *Iz-pod glyb*) in November 1974 in *samizdat*. Soon after it was also published in Russian by the YMCA Press (Paris, 1974). The English language edition was published by Little, Brown and Co. (Boston-Toronto, 1975), and by Wm Collins and Sons (London, 1975).

they were discussing some other document, in which aggression, instead of self-limitation, had been proposed.

I would not have needed to reply at all, had not Andrei Dmitrievich Sakharov been among the very first critics. His special position in our country and my profound respect for him make it impossible to ignore his statements. Today, while bearing in mind the arguments set forth in *From Under the Rubble*, I consider it my duty and right to offer an additional, brief response to Andrei Dmitrievich.

I am happy to note that the number of questions he and I are in agreement about today is incomparably greater than it was six years ago, when we became acquainted during the very months in which his memorandum* made its appearance. (I should like to hope that in another six years the area of our agreement will double.) The points on which we agree have already been noted in the press. Among the most important are (using Sakharov's formulation):

- the failure of socialism in Russia is a consequence not of a specific 'Russian tradition', but of the essence of socialism;
- the renunciation of 'socialist messianism', of overt and covert support of insurgencies throughout the world;
- separation of Marxism from the state;
- an end to guardianship over Eastern Europe;
- renunciation of the forcible retention of national republics within the Soviet Union;
- disarmament within broad limits;
- the liberation of political prisoners;
- ideological toleration;
- a strengthening of the family and the quality of upbringing;
- repairing 'the losses within human relationships, in people's souls'.

However, there are also some very important points of disagreement about which nothing should be left unclear. The principle one is *the role of ideology* in the USSR. Sakharov believes that Marxist ideology has almost no influence or significance: for the rulers it is simply a 'convenient façade', and their underlying

* First appeared in English in book form as *Progress, Coexistence, and Intellectual Freedom* (André Deutsch and W. W. Norton, 1968); reprinted in *Sakharov Speaks* (Wm Collins and Sons and Alfred A. Knopf, 1974). In the USSR Sakharov's memorandum began receiving wide *samizdat* circulation in the spring of 1968.

support is merely thirst for power. In no way, supposedly, is
either foreign or domestic policy determined by ideology; the
society is 'ideologically indifferent', with the 'hypocritical drivel'
merely 'taking the place of an oath of allegiance'.

And is this *hypocrisy* a mere trifle? Why, like a red-hot
electrode it has seared our souls throughout all the past fifty-five
years: throughout all the degrading 'self-criticism' of the
twenties and thirties; the public disavowals of one's own parents
and friends; the mockingly phrenetic 'volunteering of loans'
(for indigent collective-farm workers!); peoples' rejoicing in
the fact that they are under occupation (Occupation Day is a
national holiday!); the public's rejoicing at the news of arrests
and shootings; the superhuman villainous resolve of the
torturers; and the present-day obligatory loathsome lie – that
compulsory 'oath', the means by which the *obrazovanshchina* –
semi-educated intelligentsia – the 'hedge-ucated',* secretly
dreaming of freedom, obediently sustains its own slavery. Just
a few years ago even the editorial board of *Novy mir*, not to
mention a multitude of 'advanced' scientific research institutes,
in print expressed its esctasy over the occupation of Czechoslovakia and thereby committed an outrage upon its own policy
of many years' standing – and ideology is of no importance?
Tomorrow, when another event like that occurs, the hedge-
ucated will once again affirm their highest approval. Ideology
wrings out our souls like floor rags; it corrupts us and our
children; it brings us down below the level of animals – and it
is 'of no importance'? Is there anything in the Soviet Union
more repulsive? If *everyone disbelieves* in it, yet everyone sub-
mits to it, this is a sign not of the weakness of ideology, but of
its terrible pernicious power.

With the same imperious grip it has led our rulers – starting
from Lenin's pre-revolutionary 'Lessons of the Commune' that
proletarian power was to become firmly established only by

---

* *Obrazovanshchina* is a collective term coined by Solzhenitsyn in an
article in *From Under the Rubble* (entitled 'The Smatterers' in the
English edition). It is formed from the word *obrazovat*, 'to school, to
polish', and the pejorative suffix *-shchina*. Solzhenitsyn uses it to
denote the members of the present-day Soviet intelligentsia or, rather,
pseudo-intelligentsia, who have a 'third-rate outward polish' in place
of a true education. The attributive form 'hedge-' is used here as 'a
contemptuous adjunct' in its meaning of 'inferior, common, third-rate'
(*Oxford English Dictionary*).

mass shootings, and from Lenin's hate-obsessed secret letter about the destruction of the Church; continuing through the actual annihilation of *entire classes* and tens of millions of separate individuals (what power-seekers have ever needed such a hundredfold margin of assurance to establish what power?), and through collectivisation, which was economically senseless but nevertheless was an offering to be devoured by the ideological maw (it has recently been well demonstrated by Mikhail Agursky that the main purpose of collectivisation was to break the soul and ancient faith of the people). And in the recent past ideology has led our rulers to the diffusion – superfluous and needless to us – of Asian communism farther and farther south, and to the trampling of our allies the Czech people not for reasons of state, but merely because of an ideological rift.

Today, infected with the poison of this ideology, our rulers go on repeating, inevitably like buffoons, ghost-written speeches that even they themselves don't believe in (all they may understand is power, but they too are slaves of the ideology). They madly endeavour to ignite the whole world and seize it, even though this will bring about their own ruin and devastation, and even though they would be more comfortable resting on past conquests. But the ideology keeps driving them on! All the falsehood at home and expansion abroad, the justification of wars and murders ('progressive' murders under class-warranted circumstances of expedient!), and the justification of tomorrow's wars – it all rests on this ideology. And the almost mystical influence of the ideology accounts for the rapt enchantment of the West for half a century, its welcoming of our bestial cruelties: never would the entire enlightened world have become so blind, faced with a bunch of mere power-seekers.

Marxist ideology is the fetid root of present-day Soviet life, and only after we have cleansed ourselves of it can we begin our way back to humankind.

The second appreciable difference between Sakharov and me concerns the admissibility and reality of any other path of development for our country besides the sudden advent (and where it will come from is unexplainable) of total democracy. Theoretical considerations of this question can now be found in my first article (in the postscript of 1973) in *From Under the Rubble*. A practical survey of the history and prospects of democracy in Russia requires a separate examination on historical principles. As has happened in many instances, I have been falsely charged with having a total aversion to democracy in general, instead of doubts about a sudden introduction of democracy into the present-day USSR. I should like to direct my readers' attention once again to Mikhail Agursky, who in his comment on my *Letter to the Soviet Leaders* (in the *Vestnik russkogo khristianskogo studencheskogo dvizhenia*, No. 112*) writes responsibly about the extreme danger of *wars between nationalities* in our country that will drown in blood the birth of democracy, should it occur in the absence of strong authority. The conflicts between the nationalities as a result of the Soviet system are ten times more inflamed than they were in former Russia. One of the articles by Igor Shafarevich in *From Under the Rubble* is devoted to this question. Still another article in our collection traces the origin of totalitarianism not at all from the authoritarian systems that existed for centuries, without ever producing totalitarianism, but from the crisis of democracy, from the failure of irreligious humanism.

Finally, an essential lack of understanding arises between us when Sakharov, to my astonishment, accuses me of 'Great Russian nationalism', and even includes the word 'patriotism' in 'the arsenal of semi-official propaganda' (just as 'Orthodoxy' 'puts him on his guard' because 'Stalin tolerated a tamed Orthodoxy' – that is, *oppressed* it in accordance with his programme). Am I to be called a nationalist for proposing that no one be oppressed, that everyone be freed, and that we concentrate on the internal healing of the nation's wounds? What, then, is a conqueror to be called? The answer might be sought in the general confusion of the terms imperialism, intolerant chauvinism, arrogant nationalism, and modest patriotism (loving service to one's nation and country with sincere repentance of her sins – Sakharov himself comes within this definition). However, anyone who is well acquainted with present conditions within the Soviet social environment will agree that it is not a question of confusion in terms but of exceptionally inflamed feelings.

In my Nobel Lecture I stated in the broadest manner:

* *Herald of the Russian Student Christian Movement*, published in Russian in Paris.

'Nations are the wealth of mankind, its generalised personalities. The least among them has its own special colours and harbours within itself a special facet of God's design.' This statement was received with universal approval: a general obeisance pleasing to everyone. But as soon as I drew the conclusion that it applies to the Russian people *too*, that the Russian people *also* have a right to national consciousness, to a national rebirth in the wake of the most excruciating spiritual illness, this was furiously labelled great power nationalism. This is the vehemence not of Sakharov personally, but of the broad stratum of the educated class whose spokesman he has involuntarily become. Russians are not supposed to be able to love their own people without hating others. We Russians are forbidden to breathe a word not only about national rebirth, but even about 'national consciousness' – even this is declared a dangerous hydra.

Now that *From Under the Rubble* has appeared, I can refer to the high moral argument of Vadim Borisov, who reminds us about the nation-as-personality within the hierarchy of personalities of the Christian cosmos; that it is not history which creates nations, but nations which create history throughout their long lives, at times in light, at times in darkness, while seeking to express their personality to the fullest extent. The suppression of this personality is a most grievous sin. (For me as a writer the fate of language also hangs in the balance: if national consciousness is suppresesd, then mustn't language too, after all, be slain as a witness to the national soul? This slaying of the Russian language has in fact been going on for decades in the USSR.) Another of my co-authors, Mikhail Agursky, who can by no means be accused of bias, has recently pointed out that the present-day 'nationalism' of a large nation is a self-defence against its own expansion – which leads to the exhaustion and degeneration of primarily that nation itself. Yes, the Russian impulse towards national consciousness today is the defensive cry of a drowning people. Don't look at the outward successes of the power of the state: as a nation we Russians are in the abyss of ruin and are still looking for something we can use to grab on to and pull ourselves out.

What especially piqued Sakharov in my *Letter* and offended readers who share his view was my reference to 'the incomparable suffering borne by the Russian and Ukrainian peoples'.

I would be delighted if that phrase were without foundation. However, I wish to remind Andrei Dmitrievich that 'the horrors of the Civil War' afflicted all nationalities to an extent that was far from being 'equal'; it was mainly the Russian and Ukrainian nationalities that were afflicted. It was in *their* body that the revolution and the deliberately aimed Bolshevik terror raged. Most of the present-day Soviet republics were estranged, and the rest of the small peoples were for a time spared and supported in accordance with Communist tactics and were put to use against the great bulk. Under the pretence of annihilating the nobility, the clergy, and the merchant class it was most of all Russians and Ukrainians who were annihilated. It was most of all *their* villages that were subjected to destruction and terror by armed food-requisitioning detachments (composed mainly of outside minorities). It was on *their* territory that more than a hundred peasant uprisings were suppressed, including the extensive risings in Tambov province* and Siberia†. It was *they* who died in the great artificially created Bolshevik famines of 1921 in the Volga region and of 1931–1932 in the Ukraine. It was essentially *they* who were driven out in a throng of ten to fifteen million to die in the flat wastes under the pretext of 'dispossessing the kulaks'. (Even now there is no village poorer than a Russian village.) Indeed, Russian culture was suppressed earlier and more decisively than any other: the whole of the old intelligentsia ceased to exist; the country was swept with an epidemic of name changes as if it were under occupation; license was given in the press to scoff at both Russian folklore and the art of Palekh‡. Lenin's 'chauvinistic Great Russian riffraff' bred a further wave of unimpeded derision. *Rusopyatstvo*§ was considered a term of literary elegance. In print Russia was proclaimed a spectre, a corpse, and poets exulted:

> We shot fat-arsed Mama Russia
> For the Messiah-Communism to
> come, stepping over her body.

* 1920–1921.
† 1921.
‡ Palekh: a settlement about 170 miles north-east of Moscow famed for its icon-painting since the sixteenth century. After the Russian revolution, the artisans of Palekh adapted their techniques and style to lacquer-work based mainly on folk motifs.
§ A vernacular pejorative for Russian chauvinism.

(If bibliographic elaboration is needed, I will provide it publicly.)

And so the storm raged for some fifteen years, and no one anywhere, either in our country or abroad, suggested or even uttered a word that there existed any 'oppression of nationalities' in the Soviet Union. Only at the end of the thirties, when the two largest peoples had already been killed off and in accordance with shifting socialist tactics (superbly revealed now by Igor Shafarevich) the time had come to transfer the pressure to the small peoples, only then did we start hearing about oppression of nationalities in the USSR, which moreover was absolutely true.

I shall not go into the secondary differences of opinion between Andrei Dmitrievich Sakharov and myself as to whether one can believe, as he does, in: 'the scientific and democratic management of the economy', something not yet accomplished even in the European Economic Community; convergence;* the priority of emigration over all other rights of the people who remain; and the prosperity of Russia resulting from an influx of foreign capital (as though investors will be seeking our prosperity instead of their own quick, short-term advantage with no regard for our natural environment). I shall not reciprocate his charges of utopianism: in our helpless situation how can we not give utopia a try too now and then?

However, one cannot but marvel that in the course of replying to me Sakharov has been extremely careless in his interpretation of my point of view. He imputes to my project a 'retardation of international scientific contacts', 'ideological isolationism', an 'endeavour to fence off our country from trade ... from the exchange of people and ideas', 'communal organisation of production', 'turning over the resources of the state and the results of scientific research ... to enthusiasts inspired with a national-religious idea and creating high incomes for them ... ', and so forth. Anyone who takes the trouble to reread my *Letter* will be convinced that it contains nothing of the sort.

This vehemence and impetuosity of the pen, uncharacteristic of Sakharov, expresses the vehemence and rashness of that stratum which cannot without anger hear the words 'Russian national rebirth'.

* Of the socialist and capitalist systems.

From Under the Rubble explains how we envisage this rebirth: by travelling our path of repentance, self-limitation, and inner development, and by making our contribution to beneficent relations between peoples, without which no 'pragmatic diplomacy' and no UN vote will save humanity from destruction.

A Cycle of Poems

ALEXANDER GALICH

An Attempt at Nostalgia

...When they were driving across the Neva, Pushkin asked jokingly:

'You're sure you're not taking me to the fortress?'

'No,' replied Danzas. 'It's just that the shortest way to Chornaya Rechka goes past there.'

> Taken down by V. A. Zhukovsky from the words of Danzas, Pushkin's second.*

> ... It was last February time,
>   Every so often
> The table bore a candle's flame ...
> BORIS PASTERNAK†

> ... Pussy, keep away, an owl's
> Embroidered on the pillow.
> ANNA AKHMATOVA‡

I regret not a thing, I regret not one thing in the slightest,
Neither frontiers nor years have dominion over my heart!
So then why should I fly into panic at just the idea
That I'll never again, that I'll never, no, never, oh God ...
Just a moment, calm down, try and think –
If it's never – what then?

* Chornaya Rechka (literally 'The Black Brook'): the site of Pushkin's fatal duel, in the northern suburbs of St Petersburg. The route from Pushkin's apartment goes past the Peter-Paul fortress, in Tsarist times a place of confinement for particularly important political prisoners.
† A quotation, slightly adapted, from *Winter Night*, one of the poems of Doctor Zhivago.
‡ The opening couplet of a short poem written from a child's point of view and expressing fear of the unknown.

Arctic latitudes and their snowstorms,
Tarkhany, Vladimir, Irpen* –
So much that we never got down to,
Too late, surely, for cursing ourselves?

Our strength's ebbing more every moment,
Although our guilt isn't guilt.
Over system-built Russia the moon's out –
Number patch on a prisoner's suit.

And all those government buildings
Blood-blistered by snow and rain.
Blind-eye cataracts at their windows –
(For ages alone and friendless)
Faceless faces of leaders of men.

These wolves in their smoke-filled chambers
Lash at people as if they were dogs,
Then these wolves reach the end of their labours,
Into black limousines they clamber
And light their imported fags.

These stars of the artisan quarters
Hole up in their state-owned retreats,
And gun-toting ugly-mug warders
Will see that they can't be seen.

And then in a stoked-up sauna
These hirsute tribesmen will jig . . .
You're not sorry for these things, surely?
Not sorry at all, not one bit! . . .

And I swear that I'll never remember the years of my
    childhood,
The coast at Sebastopol – infancy's shifting truth . . .
That mysterious hill where the Chersonese slopes to a quarry,
The descant of Hellas' dust on a child's sailor suit!
I swear I'll forget! . . .
But what won't I forget? . . .

* Tarkhany, Vladimir, Irpen: notorious prisons in provincial Russia.

What won't I forget? That repulsive
Sarcastic bureaucrat's face,
The clumsiness of my hurrying,
My final pathetic rage.

I've no faith in sighing for birch trees,
You shouldn't weigh partings in tears,
And where should this debit be charted,
Is the debit side where it should be?

We stand like a petrified forest,
Struck dumb, we wait on that shore
Where the body seems not to be body,
And words are not deeds any longer,
They're not even words any more!

Left behind by the generations,
Who dismiss us as they pass;
Derision, derision, derision,
Handed us like a new gift of vision,
Passport to our future at grass!

But the horses? Those winged horses
That strain from their stone pedestals,
The hunters whistling like outlaws,
The miniature bells of the sleighs?

Yuletide holidays? Fringe of a headscarf
Falling warm on a woman's breast?
You're not sorry to leave these things, are you?
Not very . . . Well, maybe a bit!

But the candle of February's melting,
But owls on the pillow sleep,
But there's still the Chornaya Rechka,
But there's still the Chornaya Rechka,
But there's still the Chornaya Rechka,
Don't talk about that, shut up!

A Conjuration of Good and Evil

In this window the morning light breaks every day,
Like a blind man, I know everything here by touch . . .
I am leaving this house, I am leaving this house,
I am leaving this house that doesn't exist!

It's a house and it isn't, it's smoke without fire,
It's a dusty mirage or it's Fata Morgana.
And jackbooted Good with the butt of his pistol
Used to rap on my door, keeping me under guard.

And cavalier Evil would wander beside me,
He'd repulse all attempts at breaking and entering,
And the saucepan and coffee-pot there on the gas-ring
Just got on with their jobs without playing the fool!

All entangled were Evil, Indifference, Good,
In a Moscow apartment the song of a cricket,
A whole year of grace in this world without gladness,
What man would deny things were going my way?

I can sing what I want, I can shout what I want,
I go clothed in this grace like a fitted-out beggar . . .
Never mind if these clothes made my gait a bit awkward –
I chose them myself for myself, to my size.

But the reason for Good's being Good, need I say,
Is to know how to feign being good and courageous,
To deem black to be white when the circumstance favours,
And to turn into silver the blithe mercury.

All is privy to Good, all is under Good's rule,
But don't look for a lot from this noble hero,
I could gladly run from him without glancing backward,
And dig myself deep into any bolthole! . . .

First to yield was the coffee pot, bursting to bits,
Flooding the gas-rings and making foul odours . . .
Up came Good in his thundering jackboots and shouted
That cavalier Evil's to blame for it all!

Next morning Good's agent came round to our door,
He was wearing (I fancied!) the cape of a policeman . . .
Just try running from *that* without glancing backward,
Find a bolthole to flee to from *that*, just you try! . . .

And this Agent informed us, deferential but stern,
That OVIR* deals with questions of leaving the country,
That to live in our flat Evil hadn't a permit,
And one day was sufficient for packing our bags! . . .

So goodbye, my dear Evil, good Evil of mine,
Scalding candle-wax spatters the lines of the psalter.
A whole year of grace in this world without gladness,
What man would deny things were going my way?

So farewell and forgive! The grain's swollen ripe,
The shipwrights are fixing the tar-coated planking,
And it's tears and not wax on the lines of the psalter,
In our glasses there sparkles the wine of farewell.

I have tended this cornfield for two thousand years,
Isn't it time I was hastening to bring in my harvest?
Don't be sad, for it's only for ever I'm going –
Leaving Good and this house – that doesn't exist! . . .

Odessa Memories

> . . . Were it not for Helen,
> What's Troy to you, O men of Achaea?
> MANDELSTAM†

So you've learned how to play the fiddle then?
Saw that gut!
Plain-clothes Syoma yells 'Thanks a million!'
Sounds like 'Shoot!'

---

* Visa and registration department.
† From Mandelstam's lyric 'Insomnia. Homer. Taut Sails' (1915).

Syoma's out on the town with his lady friend,
Drunk and pleased.
This here lady, what do we make of her?
She's no peach!

Dark blue ribbon on ginger pony-tail,
Awf'ly chic!
All the same, in David Oistrakh's company
I'm just nix!

But when Oistrakh plays it would never do
To drink cheap wine,
In this world everything is relative –
Einstein's right.

What we get in this life's on tenterhooks –
Joy and pain.
A sharp and B flat are fundamentally
Just the same.

There's so much that's been made and overmade,
Overspill!
And so much has been known and overknown,
Heaven and hell!

. . . So come on then, Lyubov Davydovna,
Off you go then, Lyubov Davydovna,
It's your solo, Lyubov Davydovna,
One – zwei – drei!
Smells and sadness filling the speakeasy,
Heart, perish!
One good thing, it's not like the West, where come
Midnight – sssshh!
Midnight means you can snatch a snort or two,
Oh, my Lord!
Get your patents off, haul on your outside shoes,
And – off home!

... I'm on my way home. I'm very tired and I want to
Sleep, they say that when at night people
Dream they're flying, it means that
They're growing. I'm not young, but
Almost every night I
Dream I'm flying.

... My dragonfly wings so lightly
Are trembling in winds that pass,
The green wedges of the pine trees
Beneath me rustle like grass.

And on to – Thalassa, Thalassa,
Creation's enchanted stay,
I'm only a ten-year-old lad now
But I really do know how to fly!

It's no fairy tale, I'm flying really,
Through the mists before dawning day,
Over boats with their varied rigging
And the city that's always grey,

Over dusty omnibus depots –
To the land that lives evermore,
Where again the Achaean elders
Make ready their vessels for war.

Another man's senseless grieving
Bids them bend their oars against Troy,
But I must beyond the Aegean,
I still have further to grow.

I'll grow to be brave and virile,
I'll accept the world like a prize,
And a girl in a dark blue ribbon
Will nestle up to my side,

Once more in the ruins of Ilium
The trumpet will call Helen's name,
And once more . . .

At the corner of Sadovaya Street three men stopped me.
They knocked my hat off. Laughing, they asked:
'Haven't you gone to Israel yet, you old git?'
'What d'you mean, what d'you mean? I'm at home,
I'm at home — so far. I still fly in my sleep. I'm
still growing.'

Cough Your Throat Clear, February

Cough your throat clear, February, blast your blizzards,
Let your frosts crack down, unleashed from their traces,
We've been prodigal with our prometheanism,
Primogeniture we've passed unsuspecting!

Let's console ourselves with hospital wards, then,
And the way we never could make our minds up,
We've so gorged ourselves on dishwater pottage,
That we've never managed yet to get our breath back!

Listening to Bach

My guitar on the wall started sounding,
And the wallpaper flowers flared.
Isolation that God's gift imposes —
So lovely, and so hard to bear!

In this world what could be more lovely —
(It spites all the plagues of this life!)
Isolation of sound and colour,
The fall of a final line?

And fancy sets out on its journey
To the point where it becomes fact . . .
Who would dare to command the Lord God
And seek to control His paths?

The words that a verse line sculpted,
The canvas transformed into mist –
It's so easy to stretch and touch them,
The temptation's so hard to resist!

Lordly hangmen have no comprehension
That not all kinds of closeness are close,
The D minor Toccata's a temple,
And their permits won't open its doors! . . .

Encounter with Milovan Djilas

CARL-GUSTAV STRÖHM

The house stands in a quiet side street of Belgrade, not far from the Parliament building. Tall trees give shade. Some housewives are carrying their afternoon purchases. A little cluster of men, in deep conversation. The entrance opens on a hallway characteristic of the thirties, with the slightly faded look typical of the socialist tenement house. A brass plate engraved in cyrillic lettering: MILOVAN DJILAS. A mistrustful housekeeper (or is she a relative?) opens the door just a crack. But then at last he is standing before me: the one-time professional communist revolutionary, leader of the partisans during World War II, friend and close collaborator of Marshal Tito, rebel for and against communism, the man who sacrificed political power and a brilliant career for the sake of truth, to spend years in the prisons of the same state which he himself had fought, gun in hand, to establish.

Since the last time I saw him, his hair has turned ice grey. Strange, what the years will do to some people's faces. Some faces grow hard, bitter, but not that of Djilas. On the contrary, the former guerrilla leader and Communist functionary, the terror of the intellectuals of Belgrade and Zagreb, has been mellowed by suffering. The hard look in some of the photographs of him as a youth, as a partisan, is gone. His gaunt figure reminds one of the frescoes found on the walls of ancient Serbian and Montenegrin abbeys. The former hero has turned into a sage. But his eyes have kept their fire, bearing witness to a youth spent in struggle and revolution.

He invites me into his study: a desk, a bed, books on shelves covering the wall. There is a manuscript on the table. It is his latest book, he says; its subject is genocide, the murder of peoples. It deals specifically with the slaughter of the Mohammedan population of Montenegro by the Christian Orthodox inhabitants in the wake of the First World War. Djilas, a man who has himself taken an active part in history and politics, is concerned with the problem of guilt – and he concludes that in such fateful times as these, general guilt cannot be determined, i.e., it does not exist. There are too many factors involved, too much that is incalculable, too many passions, to allow for a superficial answer to that question.

It shows that Milovan Djilas did not stop half-way in his departure from Communist ideology. He has suffered in his own flesh the inherently tragic nature of human action and inaction. He knows in his bones that there are no simple answers. Does Djilas believe in God? No, he says, religion plays no part in his thinking. If there is a God, he, Djilas, cannot believe that such a higher being would concern himself with the trivia and pettiness of human existence.

Perhaps this heroic agnosticism is a legacy of his native land, Montenegro: a country in which the bishops were warriors and the warriors bishops, and where Christianity was one aspect of the struggle against domination by the occupying Turks.

We then spoke about Solzhenitsyn, about the book *Gulag Archipelago*, which Djilas has read from cover to cover. He fetches his copy from the desk, to show me all the places he has carefully underlined in pencil. This, he says, is the most significant book of our times. Solzhenitsyn was as close to him, Djilas, as almost anyone. Here for the first time the nature of Communist ideology has been exposed in its entirety. When I asked him whether he would like to engage in discussion with Solzhenitsyn, as Sakharov has done, Djilas shakes his head. It was enough that the whole force of the Soviet Union, the KGB, and the Communist parties of the world, had attacked Solzhenitsyn. No, Djilas will not utter a word of criticism against this man. One senses something of the ancient bond between the Montenegrins and the peoples of Russia in Djilas – and also something of partisan comradeship. He leaps to the defence of his friend and comrade Solzhenitsyn without asking questions first.

The Communists, Djilas says, have made the fatal mistake of continuing with a revolution which cannot be carried on in the circumstances of today. Their efforts to keep communism alive had to run aground, because the historical situation that gave it birth has come to an end. All they now have left is the outward show of power, and their habitual dealing in concepts that have long ago lost their meaning. Yet Djilas, who is ostracised by his former ideological associates in Yugoslavia and refused a passport (at a time when most other citizens of Yugoslavia can get them) never comes out with any general condemnation. The respect with which he speaks of Tito is noteworthy. He regards Tito's foreign policy as the only one possible and right for Yugoslavia. On another occasion Djilas had said that Tito understood the Soviet leaders and their methods as hardly any other statesman outside the Warsaw Pact nations did. Is it possible that in these words from the political pensioner Milovan Djilas there is an undertone of nostalgia for the vanished years of struggle and enthusiasm?

Djilas's view of the West is not at all pessimistic. He considers current unpleasant developments in Western society – from criminality to pornography – as mere fringe manifestations. They are not central, he says, nor do they alter the fact that the Western form of life is far superior to Communism.

Today Djilas lives like a stranger in his own country. It seems there are people who are afraid to speak with him. He is subjected – especially on the lower levels – to all kinds of insidious and petty insults. Nevertheless, Milovan Djilas looks to the future with confidence. He does not pine for the power he once held. If he had cared about power, he says, his life would have taken a different course. Politics, says this man steeped for so long in them, is in a sense always a dirty business. Everything depends on whether the active politician has a code of ethics, a morality, that can give meaning to his actions and limit the arbitrariness of power.

Writing, he says, in concluding the interview, does not come as easily now as it did in earlier years. Still, it looks as though this man, familiar now with the life of contemplation as with the life of action has not yet had his last say by a long shot. Out of the hardship and poverty of Balkan life, out of the turmoils of civil war, a man has come up who disseminates wisdom and goodness to all around him. Quite apart from anything else, the world is indebted to him merely for setting such an example.

Remarks on the 'Metaphysical Situation'

ALEXANDER PIATIGORSKY

This is a short article – no more than an impression. And by no means the first. More likely the last. Not because the things I am about to discuss will change so much as to become unrecognisable, but rather because one changes oneself, and soon I shall not be able to see them with the same eyes.

A friend of mine living in England once asked me: 'Do you think that the metaphysical ideas current in Russia today are really important?' I replied: 'No, of course not.' But the very fact that metaphysical ideas are to be found at all in Russia today is extremely interesting. After all, in earlier years, when one would have thought many of the external conditions were much more favourable, there was no metaphysical thinking going on, or very little (as in the short quarter century after Solovyev*). Yet today there is a strange profusion of it.

The forms of this thinking are highly eccentric and ephemeral. Metaphysics is not taught in universities, no work is done on it at research institutes, learned societies do not debate it, scholarly journals do not devote articles to it, and metaphysicians give no talks on radio and television.

Yet it would be quite wrong to say that Russian metaphysics lives underground. Not at all! Its element is neither above nor below ground. Like much else in Russia, it exists in some curious 'no man's land' of Russia's spiritual and intellectual life.

One old man I know has lectured all his life on electronics at some institute, and at the same time has been conducting an unending series of seminars at his home on 'Plato, Hegel,

* V. S. Solovyev (1853–1900), famous in Russia as a religious writer, philosopher, and mystical poet. *Author*.

Christianity and our life'. Moreover, these were no mere fire-side chats. The seminars began in 1949 and ran with only one interruption (when one of its main organisers fell seriously ill) till 1971. It did not even suspend its activities over summer holidays. After the death of its founder it turned out that the seminar's records amounted to about thirty thousand printed pages. Another 'leading metaphysician' (still alive, thank God) teaches Marxist philosophy (dialectical and historical material-ism) at one of the industrial institutes. Having given a routine lecture on, say, 'The Primacy of Matter and the Secondary Nature of Consciousness', he would make for a chemist friend's *dacha* and there give a lecture on 'The Illusory Nature of the Material World and the Reality of Conscious Being'. A third example is an artist living near Moscow who for twenty years has conducted a seminar on 'Occultism and Godmanhood'. These occasions are all quite unofficial. But there are other kinds too. Once I was rung up by the trade union committee of an aircraft-building institute and was asked to give a lecture on the philosophy of Buddhism. Just before the start of the lecture (about two hundred scientists, engineers and technicians had gathered for it), a member of the trade union committee came up to me (as I discovered afterwards, he was secretary of the primary party organisation) and said, 'Please, Alexander, do tell us about things that *we can't read anywhere*. We are fed up with all that . . .' (there followed an unprintable epithet which aptly summed up the state of affairs in official philosophy). Or to take another example (a clear case of 'no man's land'): after a general lecture on India of a kind which the authorities of my institute sometimes asked me to give, the organisers (I think it was at one of the Moscow chemical works) plied me with food and drink and for four whole hours literally interrogated me about how it was possible to 'reconcile' (a favourite modern – and not only modern – expression which perfectly charac-terises 'no man's land') religion with positive scientific know-ledge.

However that may be, metaphysicians are *talking* and *writing*. They are talking not so much at seminars as among their metaphysician friends. They are writing not for publication, but simply in order not to forget their thoughts. And it must not on any account be supposed that for them metaphysics 'satisfies intellectual hunger' or 'fills up life's emptiness'. These are people who are intellectually already extremely active, and their lives are only too full without metaphysics. Pure speculation and free philosophising is their destiny, and it leads them away from the conformism of the majority, as well as from the oppositional activity of the minority.

Here I should like to outline just a few of the ideas which are exercising Russian (the word indicates a country only: metaphysics knows no nation!) and especially Moscow metaphysicians today. The problem which has meant most to them in recent years is that of gaining a *full understanding of their own situation*. But what, one may ask, does the word 'situation' mean, if nothing is *happening* in metaphysics, if there is no *development*, no *process*. (Incidentally, this approach reflects perfectly the transitional nature, the ephemerality, of the life of the Russian metaphysician, although perhaps, as my English friend remarked, it is precisely these everyday 'circumstantial' peculiarities of Russian existence which stimulate metaphysical thought, and but for them the electrical engineer would happily stick to his electrical engineering, like everyone else, the chemist would remain a chemist, and the professor of Marxism would give lectures on metaphysics without being any kind of metaphysician in real life, although then his other, 'non-metaphysical', life would be not ephemeral but solidly based on reality.) In any event, 'situation' means essentially one thing to the metaphysicians with whom I have frequently discussed it (despite all the shades of interpretation they give to it): the processes and developments which can take place in people who are drawn by metaphysical ideas and concepts, who find themselves inside the gravitational field of the impersonal conscious force. (I mean, of course, a field wholly impervious to the individual or social characteristics of those who are 'drawn into' it from outside.) The Moscow psychologist M., who has been working recently on metaphysics (and phenomenology) put it like this (in one of his *unpublished* articles): 'The impersonal conscious force always affects the mentality, the psychological make-up, the memory, thinking and behaviour of those who are 'drawn into' its gravitational field. And the deeper they are inside that field, the more precisely their language grasps it, and the more strongly that impersonal force affects them.'

Since the end of the 1960s it has been more and more clearly realised in Russia that metaphysics is absolutely alien to any kind of 'natural' specifications, that is, to peculiarities generated by the natural world. It knows no homeland, no country, no race and no nation, but its field of influence, as it has come and is coming into operation in people, is not only the space in which they *live* but also that in which they *have lived*.

The origins of the 'metaphysical situation' lie in two very important *historical* (not metaphysical!) circumstances. Firstly: by the beginning of the nineteenth century in Russia philosophy had already been unnaturally (not to say perversely) divided into *religious*, that is, derived from an experience of prayer, meditation and theology growing out of tradition, and *secular*, that is, drawing continually from recent (and later on contemporary) European philosophy.* I say 'unnatural' here not as an ethical evaluation. (Though it is part of my conception that any pure philosophical activity is *already* religious in nature, even in the non-specific sense of the word, and even in the unreduced understanding of the concept, and consequently I hold that any such division causes artificial spiritual discord among thinking people, and hence the fruitless expenditure of spiritual energy.)

Secondly: from the time that western philosophy (whether metaphysical or any other kind – mostly 'any other kind', in fact) began to be regularly assimilated, that assimilation (however earnestly it might claim to be theoretical and concerned with the truth alone) was coloured by expediency, by the use of philosophy to solve the problems of the moment, and above all by expediency of a social and cultural type. Philosophy was always relevant (or irrelevant, which comes to the same thing) to something or other, or (at best) was held to have arisen as a result of something or other. One moment it was a 'justification of existing reality', at another moment 'a condemnation of existing reality', at a third 'a weapon in the struggle' or 'a grounds for compromise'. The negative aspect always held the upper hand over the positive, and everyone was constantly getting bogged down in quarrels and mutual recriminations, searching for each others' mistakes and arguing the toss over

* One might add that, because of the purely historical circumstances of Russia the first always remained alien to the official church, and the second to official scholarship. *Author.*

who was right and who was wrong – all of this without really undertaking any profound *personalised philosophical work*. No sooner had someone become an adherent of some philosophical idea, than he would turn it into a means of group identity, into an instrument (or emblem) for counterposing the 'we' (not the 'I') of one group to the 'they' of another.

The 'philosophic fever' would regularly grip Russia's thinkers, quite independent of their talent or lack of it: the Hegelian ravings of Belinsky,* Herzen and Bakunin, the Feuerbachian cretinism of Chernyshevsky, the anti-Catholicism of Dostoyevsky and the 'everyday didacticism' of Tolstoy are in that sense reflections of one and the same profound lack of religious and metaphysical seriousness.† It is hardly surprising that in this atmosphere of absorption in socially expedient superficialities philosophically active people knew virtually nothing about the life and death of Seraphim of Sarov (Belinsky's contemporary!) and did not begin to grasp the philosophical significance of Vladimir Solovyev. Who knows, perhaps these things were also the result of a certain lack of philosophical professionalism and of respect for that peculiar profession – for profession it is: the philosopher is not only he who wants to and can philosophise, but also he who (quite apart from wanting) can hardly do anything else.‡

Major changes in the metaphysical situation came about with the wave of cultural rebirth of the late 1890s to 1910s. The thinking of Rozanov, Bulgakov, Florensky, Berdyaev, Shestov and a few other religious thinkers was marked by an intensive philosophical re-evaluation and reconceptualisation of Christian ideas, by the restoration of philosophy to its natural religious underpinnings, by the transition to a truly free form of

---

* Vissarion Belinsky (1811–1848) was the father of Russian socially orientated literary criticism and is a major influence on today's Russian intelligentsia.

† It is very amusing that the young Nabokov in *The Gift* saw only half the truth: for him Chernyshevsky and Dostoyevsky were at opposite poles in respect of 'the gift'. He did not perceive that they are twin brothers in their monism, intolerance and hatred of absolute freedom. *Author.*

‡ It is the presence of a professional corpus of philosophy and the phenomenal degree of respect accorded to it which explains the fact that Seraphim's younger contemporary, Ramakrishna, was properly understood in 'poverty-stricken India'. *Author.*

philosophising which rejected (at least in intention) social and cultural expediency, and by the search for new forms and structures through which to convey traditional ideas. What is especially important about them for our epoch (that is, for our situation) is that their works, being saturated with Russian Orthodox concepts, proved an excellent exemplar not only for the transmission of Orthodoxy, but for the imparting of religious ideas in general.

The subsequent secular persecution of the Orthodox faith in the twenties and thirties, the official revival of Orthodoxy which replaced it in the forties, and finally the 'religious liberalism' of the fifties and early sixties had one very strange and completely unforeseen consequence (unforeseen not because it was impossible to foresee it, but because there was *nobody* to foresee it): serious thinking people began to discover from their own thought processes that any *consistent* philosophical activity leads inevitably to religious metaphysics.

On one occasion Sh. indulged in the following comparison: 'All individual denominational religions are the various instruments of the divine orchestra. Wouldn't it be absurd if the violinist, instead of playing his instrument, started to beat the horn player over the head with his bow, insisting that all music was for the violin? Yet that is what people have been doing and are still doing. And that is not the fault of the violin, but of the violinist, because he does not yet (or has ceased to) realise he is a *musician*. His playing has not yet reached the level of *real musicianship*.' Various perceptions of this situation are possible, and most of them would be right. In the early sixties one close colleague of mine, R., a theoretical linguist, in reply to my question whether he was convinced of the existence of God, said: 'For me precise positive knowledge is a matrix which cannot exist without at least one empty cell. That cell is God.' What is noteworthy here is that R. turned my question on its head: like a true scholar he was convinced, not that God exists, but that science cannot exist without Him, just as he (R.) cannot exist without science. That demonstrates the metaphysical pluralism of R. (who later became one of the leading semiotic theorists).

Many scholars of a positivist frame of mind began to evolve towards a metaphysical position *unconsciously* (simply through *natural* consistency in their thinking), and that nearly always came about through *abandoning* some single viewpoint, through a release from *monism*. In this sense one fact is particularly significant: scholars would often come to the concept of God as a result of a critical analysis of the language of their own concepts. The major characteristic of contemporary metaphysical thinking in Russia is a peculiar understanding of the problem of 'self-identification' as it stands in relation to the problem of 'naming' ('self-identification' meaning here the act of identifying oneself with a certain abstract position, while 'naming' refers to the 'label' for that position).

'Naming' exists on two levels: the 'zero' level, when no actual name is given at all, and the 'mystical' level, when one is given one's name not merely as one among many, but by the Divine Power and as one individual and irreplaceable *you*. It must be said that my attitude to 'naming' (on both the 'zero' and 'mystical' levels) was formed under the very strong influence of Sh. and P. It was while conversing with them (each separately) that I became aware of the possibility of reducing the *very concept* of 'naming' to certain elementary constituents of consciousness. Thus, talking of naming on the mystical level Sh. said: 'God's naming a personality by its own name means that that personality is not and cannot be aware of itself (or identify itself) as a separate personality, as an "I", for as a personality or individual it is already conatively dissolved in the Divine Purpose and Will, and knows that its "I" does not exist.' P. said, 'For me names like Socrates, Descartes and Kant are simply symbols or names of the impersonal Conscious Force which, continually swirling, eddying and sparkling, crystallises itself at the points in space and time which we call Socrates, Descartes and Kant.'

About a year ago the linguist T., after an hour's conversation on Buddhist metaphysics, said to me, 'I am an Orthodox believer, but only from a non-existent, abstract standpoint. Or, to put it another way, if the head of my institute were to ask me what I believe, then I should tell him that I am an Orthodox believer, but if a priest were to ask me, then I should have to tell him simply that I am baptised, for I must assume that a priest possesses (whether he actually does or not I cannot know) a level of religious and mystical insight from which I am clearly an unbeliever'. Interpreting that statement in the light of theology, Sh. replied with a paraphrase from Nikita Stiphates (a late Byzantine saint): 'They are none of them baptised, but are catechumen', having in mind merely the symbolic form and not the mystical communion indicated by the words 'believer', 'baptised', in so far as they are not submitted to verification by metaphysical thought. The principle operating on this level may look like extreme rationalism, but to my mind it is, rather, another version of the ancient Buddhist concept (wholly mystical in nature – that is, accessible to cognition only in the experience of special states of consciousness) of the 'emptiness of all concepts', and it reminds one also of the Christian concept of apophatic experience. But the principle does not necessarily spring from denominational religion. During a long discussion on the language of metaphysics, the well-known mathematical logician V. said: 'You know what strikes me? Our anti-religious propaganda proclaims that "there is no God". But you notice that no Christian text actually states that "there is a God", but rather that "God is a Trinity".' He was pointing out that, metaphysically speaking the official atheist standpoint *has no language*, or, putting it in Buddhist terms, one could say that it has no language *capable of being verified: its 'language' is merely a means of describing the atheist reaction to something which it calls religion*. In the last analysis, the statement 'you believe in God, but I am an atheist' is as metaphysically meaningless as the statement 'you are an atheist but I believe in God', for both convey a certain negativist outlook, which is wholly incompatible with free religious and metaphysical thinking.

The last point is very important. The Russian metaphysical situation 'cut its teeth' at the same time (especially in Moscow) as a wave of conversions to Christianity, Judaism, and Buddhism was taking place. To my mind this was no 'coincidence', but a common impulse which produced different effects on different human (personal) material. However, a denominational religion gives the individual who does not verify his own thinking much greater opportunity for labelling himself than does metaphysics. Quite recently, a Moscow physicist, A.V., after I had fruitlessly tried several times to tap a vein of metaphysical thinking in him, said to me, 'You know, Alexander, it would be an excellent thing, if you, as a Buddhist, would explain to us Jews how you see the present position of the Jews in our country.' My first reaction was: 'But, good heavens, for me, as a Buddhist, there can be no such thing as a Russian, or a Jew, or even a country, let alone a position. And for them as Jews, how can anything exist but the Torah and the Lord's Will? What can I tell them?' But then I reflected: 'But, my goodness! I am a Buddhist as much as they are Jews. We are drowning in the labels we attach to ourselves. Perhaps they do not realise that I am a Jew and they are Buddhists.'*

But this is the whole point, that here we are dealing with an existential need to define our own identity, a need which can be reflected in religion. It is this kind of reflection which, in the metaphysical situation existing in Moscow since the early sixties, has led to an ever sharper division of theoretical thinkers into methodologists, systematisers and pure metaphysicians, a division which (thank God!) has never received organisational form, but which has always had its absolutely clear personal motivation.

Metaphysicians realise that naming is fatal, for it always turns into labelling at the expense of self-knowledge. They also realise that reflection (even in the early stages of religious insight) helps the individual to become, to turn himself into, a personality. P. expressed that idea very aptly in roughly the following words: 'The ordinary person *knows* that he is Russian, Jewish, a believer or an atheist, but if he *works* unremittingly, then he will no longer know it, indeed *cannot* know it, like someone who for long has not *heard* what others are naming him (for he *only reads* his thinking, that is, his "work").'

When T., at a methodological seminar, was called a 'Russian individualist', his reply amusingly (and correctly!) combined the Buddhist and phenomenological approaches. What he said was: 'I am a Russian, since a lot of people (yourselves included) call me that, and there is no reason why I should agree or

---

* Just two months later, having left the Soviet Union, I met some very pleasant, decent and likeable Jews whose one defect in my eyes was that they *knew exactly* who were Jews and who were not. According to their criterion a Jew is a person of Jewish origin who either professes Judaism or is an atheist. But if he holds any other, non-Judaic, religious beliefs, then he is *not a Jew*. My physicist was, in metaphysical terms, being much more cautious. *Author.*

disagree. But the term "individualist" has a double meaning. It can refer to a person who does not want to be confused with others (and certainly not with those who do the confusing), or, as Pomerants put it, the gentleman does not wish to be confused with the scum, that is, he wants to be an *individual*. Or the term can refer to his desire to be an individual *in order to become* a personality. Those are two quite different readings of the term.' And when Sh. asserts that there is no such thing as 'simple faith' (since it is faith we are talking about) but that there *is* 'liberating theological and doctrinal speculation', that is virtually equivalent to Berdyaev's 'existential cry' that there is only *absolute freedom* (in 'self-knowledge') and not freedom 'from something'.

The attitude of Russian metaphysicians to the problem of naming (I have not touched on the social implications of the problem here) probably shows more clearly than anything else the religious indeterminacy of the metaphysical situation in Russia. At the moment I feel this is a good thing: the less defined religious metaphysics is, the more its contact with present-day positivist science is objectively inevitable, provided that it develops consistently and correctly from its basic premises, of which the most important, to my mind, is the 'absolute relativity of language'.

The Paradoxes of the Grenoble Exhibition on Unofficial Soviet Art

IGOR GOLOMSHTOK

The exhibition of eight Moscow artists, which took place in 1974 in Grenoble, has given us a new view of so-called unofficial Soviet art. It is one thing to see these works in their natural surroundings: in Moscow, in the homes or the studios of their authors, amongst the objects of everyday life, from which they emerged and whose imprint they bear; or even less often at official exhibitions, where among the many miles of officially commissioned painting they appear as rare threads in the tattered fabric of the Russian avant-garde tradition. It is a completely different thing to see them torn from their natural surroundings and transplanted to a modern western museum.

Among the provincial museums of France, that of Grenoble is noted for its first-class collection of contemporary art and for its interest in current trends. The curators have done their best to adapt the old building, with its somewhat pompous style of the last century, to its new role. The spacious entrance hall has been modernised by a sytem of lightweight partitions, in one of which there is a round, narrow opening. On passing through this we find ourselves in a long, dark tunnel with a corrugated iron floor, and as we walk we hear the hollow echo of our own footsteps. After this solemn march through a darkness relieved only by the dim light of tiny lamps mounted on side rails, we emerge in the great hall of the former library, its walls covered with yard upon yard of panelling, decorated with an abstract geometrical design. Here works of modern art stand, hang from the ceiling, or protrude from the walls: gigantic overhead constructions of steel tubing, revolving metal sculptures, twisted iron, plastic, papier mâché, concrete – showing no sign of brushwork or chisel, the conventional mediums of art.

In the neighbouring rooms an exhibition of works by Theodor Balli was being held at the same time, and his sculptures, resembling brightly painted three-dimensional road signs, were scattered – as an advertisement of modernity – even among the paintings of old masters. So next to these, in two large well lit halls, the works of Moscow artists were on show: the crooked houses of O. Rabin, the brittle fantasies of B. Sveshnikov, the playing-card collages of V. Nemukhin, the white forms on a white background of V. Weisberg, the paintings and drawings of D. Plavinsky, A. Zverev, A. Kharitonov and D. Krasnopevtsev. Two worlds with a single date have met in the halls of the museum: the open world of western artistic culture, unrestricted by rules, free in all its manifestations, and the closed, intimate world of the Moscow artists, concentrated only on itself; the culture of matter, invention, concept, intellect and the culture of introspection, spirit, experience; steel, concrete, spray-guns, electric welding and sheets of plain paper, torn from pads, worked with oil, pen or pencils. . . .

In the eyes of the western audience, accustomed to judge art primarily by its formal innovations, the works on display at the Grenoble exhibition were certainly not avant-garde. It has all already happened in the West, so there was a tendency to see in the painting of the Moscow artists little more than the influence of expressionism, surrealism and other schools, which have already become classics of twentieth-century art. Roughly this same view is expressed by many western critics, when they write about Russian art. The Italian professor Franco Miele, in his recent important book on the subject, gives the following mortifying characterisation of the new unofficial movement in Soviet art: 'Owing to the lack of first-class talents and to the restricted field of activity of the sculptors and painters, their output is not the result of a profound internal maturity, but represents instead an indirect process of perceiving, but imprecisely and fragmentarily, western problems.'* The presence or absence of talent in contemporary unofficial Russia is a matter for debate; as for the second part of Miele's diagnosis, it is undoubtedly the result of his 'imprecise and fragmentary' understanding of the problems of Russian culture and

* Franco Miele. *L'avanguardia tradita. Arte Russo dal XIX al XX sec.* Rome, 1973.

of the reality, from which this culture grows. It seems that even thirty or so visits to the Soviet Union (of which the professor informs us) were insufficient for this purpose.

To evaluate the artistic culture of one country according to the criteria of another, and to issue on this basis a copyright in originality to one of them, is a common enough pre-occupation among the wider public, but of little use to the historian. Avant-garde cultures do occur, but alongside these other cultures too exist, maintaining close links with the past, translating the categories of old traditions into a new language. To contemporaries the first type appears progressive, while the second seems reactionary, conservative, lagging behind the age. However, the test of time often reveals that it was precisely the 'reactionary' cultures which succeeded not only in creating new values, but also in preserving something from the old, which has been lost by the 'progressives'. It is well known, for example, that in the fifteenth century the cultures of the Italian Renaissance and of Northern Europe underwent parallel development. The confusing of criteria in the assessment of these brought whole generations of historians and art historians to a critical impasse. I think that something similar is now taking place in the case of the juxtaposition of Soviet unofficial art and western culture.

This historical analogy is, of course, tenuous. Firstly, one can hardly compare the output of the handful of underground artists, working in the Soviet Union today, with the general picture of western art over the last few decades. (If, however, we consider that the number of these artists is constantly increasing, and if we do not restrict Russian artistic culture to the sphere of painting and sculpture, i.e. if we include, for instance, literature, then the above imbalance is greatly reduced.) Secondly, the very divergence between contemporary Russian and western art arose as the result of a genetic paradox: western culture, developing organically, step by step, moved towards an ever greater break with tradition, until (in its extreme manifestations) it rejected it altogether, whereas Russian culture, whose tradition has been forcibly interrupted, condemned and destroyed, gravitates in its most avant-garde form towards the extreme of traditionalism (not, of course, in the narrow Soviet sense, but in the broadest connotation of the word). Western critics are understandably perplexed when confronted with this 'illogicality'* of Russian culture.

The artists whose works were shown at the Grenoble exhibition do not exhaust the range of unofficial art in the Soviet Union. The last two decades have seen the emergence of Soviet abstractionists, creators of pure form, dealing with problems of the relationship between light, colour, volume and motion, also exponents of pop art, conceptual art and other artistic trends experienced in the West. Among them there are some very serious artists, and formally speaking it would seem they have made considerable advances. Nevertheless, I maintain that the nucleus of the movement – its nerve centre and vanguard – is represented not by the innovators of form and new creative concepts, but by those who have discovered a new vision and new interpretation of the world.

The traditionalism of contemporary Russian avant-garde is not a result of Soviet ideology, or of any compromise with this ideology, or of any desire to adapt 'fragmentarily understood' western problems to the immature tastes of the local public. This artistic paradox is in fact the organic product of the paradoxical atmosphere of the whole of Soviet reality over the last twenty years and constitutes the uniqueness of Soviet unofficial art as a social and aesthetic phenomenon.

The specific nature of this phenomenon by no means consists of its unofficial or underground character. Our suffering century has known many forms of such art, and wherever creative freedom has been suppressed by a totalitarian regime a reaction against this has arisen and found its reflection in art. In the 1930s and 1940s unofficial art became widespread in Fascist Italy. It existed deep underground in the Third Reich and in Nazi-occupied territories. It is enough to mention here the names of the German artists Ernst Barlach, Kathe Kollwitz, Hans and Lea Grundig, the early French and Italian neo-realists (Guttuso, Mucchi, Fougeron, Taslitsky), the Polish sculptor Dunikowski, and the Hungarian expressionists. They often combined their creative activity with political struggle. The stimulus and driving force behind their art

---

* Franco Miele suggests that perhaps the main negative symptom of Russian culture lies in the fact that it has no logic of development, nor any logical philosophical concept as its basis.

was a protest against the totalitarian regime and its culture.

Unlike these, the initiators of Soviet underground art were far removed from social struggle, and the products of their inspiration did not contain any political allusions, whether direct or indirect. As a socio-artistic phenomenon it came into being in the mid-1950s, a reaction not against the regime, but against the cultural and aesthetic vacuum, which had been created in the country during the long years of Stalin's rule.

The history of the foundation of this vacuum is treated by Soviet art historians as the mainstream in the development of Socialist Realism, as a stage on its great path, as its highest achievement. The first step in this direction was made by the resolution of the All-Union Communist Party, dated the 23 April 1932, 'On the Reformation of Literary-Artistic Organisations'. This abolished all artistic associations and together with these the last remnants of creative freedom in the country. Henceforth the only permitted form of art would be Socialist Realism, the essence of which was defined as 'the true depiction of reality in its revolutionary development', but with the significant reservation that the artist should look at this reality through the eyes of the ruling party (the so-called 'principle of *partiinost*' in art). And from this, by a natural process, the only right of the Soviet artist was derived – the right to eulogise the heroic deeds of the leaders and the growth in the living standards of the people. And as the famine, which was wiping out millions of peasants, grew more terrible, as Stalin's terror gained in fury, so too the harvest supper portrayed by artists on the tables of the collective farms, became more plentiful, and the faces of the workers with their painted smiles blossomed with an ever greater joy during meetings with party and government officials on the canvases of the 'true depictors of reality'. During the 1930s and 1940s anything which did not conform to the standards of Socialist Realism was viciously eradicated. For a quarter of a century not a single exhibition was organised, not a single book on foreign art was published. Between 1929 and 1937 treasures from the State Hermitage in Leningrad were sold as unwanted to foreign capitalists (fifteen out of forty Rembrandts, the best of the works by Van Eyck, Raphael, Velasquez, Titian and others). Apparently the proceeds were used for the purchase of barbed wire. In 1947 the Museum of

Modern Western Art in Moscow (one of the best collections in the world of the impressionists, Cézanne, early Picasso, Matisse and others) was shut down, and its building on Kropotkinskaya Street was taken over by the newly formed Academy of Arts of the USSR. In 1949, at the height of the campaign against cosmopolitanism, the Pushkin State Museum of Fine Arts – the only collection of classical western painting in Moscow – was closed to make room for a permanent exhibition of gifts to comrade Stalin. The exhibitions at the Tretiakov Gallery and the Russian Museum did not go beyond the Wanderers,* and during the last Stalin years even Levitan aroused suspicion by his alleged tendency towards impressionism. All this inevitably led to a sharp decline in the artistic taste of the public and in the professional standard of the artists, which one might justly term a cultural vacuum.

One can hardly speak of unofficial or underground art during the Stalin period, despite the fact that the external conditions for this existed. For the founders of Soviet avant-garde who did not accept the new official artistic ideology continued to work. However, the gap between this ideology and the whole of twentieth-century world culture was by now so large, and the level of artistic awareness in the country had fallen so low, that not only the works of Malevich and Tatlin, but even the paintings of Vrubel or Renoir were indistinguishable in the eyes of the majority from daubs on canvas by the tail of the donkey, which had become the symbolic author of all art that departed from the familiar standards of Socialist Realism. Because of the complete lack of a suitable audience, art of any other kind could not assume the character of a social phenomenon.

The fruition came only later, in the years of the so-called Khrushchev liberalisation, when the iron curtain – which had isolated the country both in space (from contemporary culture) and in time (from all the previous culture of mankind) – was slightly lifted, and the atmosphere from the other side of the curtain began to enter the vacuum. At exhibitions of foreign art, from the mid-1950s to the early 1960s (e.g. the exhibition at the Sixth World Youth and Student Festival in Moscow in

* A school of naturalistic painters critical of pre-Revolutionary Russian society, proclaimed today as the founders of officially approved socialist realism in the visual arts.

1957, at which over 4,500 works by young artists from fifty-two countries of the world were shown, also exhibitions of Picasso, Léger, of English, French and American art, of paintings from the Dresden gallery and the Louvre, and even of Mexican art), Soviet artists and public for the first time in twenty-five years were able to see the living art of the twentieth century and inhale the fresh atmosphere of its creative searching and innovation. This does not simply mean that young artists came under the pernicious influence of the West (as this phenomenon is generally regarded – through either ignorance or stupidity – by the theoreticians of Socialist Realism). The contact had much more serious consequences: the artists discovered things which had been banished from their surrounding reality, but which had continued a clandestine existence within each of them. That is, they discovered the great world of culture, to which they belonged by right of birth and from which they had been sentenced to lifelong exile by the mysterious laws governing their society, the laws of materialism.

Boris Petrovich Sveshnikov, perhaps the most important of the Moscow artists working today, used to tell the story of how on the day of his return after eight years in the camps, instead of going home or to a restaurant or to visit his friends he set off straight from the station to the Pushkin Museum. At the age of eighteen, after completing only two years at art school, he had been deported to Vorkuta. In this northern hell the artist lived by the values of world culture and saw the reality of his imprisonment in the light of these values. Sveshnikov was lucky. After two years of hard labour, which reduced him to a state of utter physical exhaustion, he succeeded in getting a job as a night watchman in the camp store and here, in secret, he began to draw. The northern scenery reminded him of the cosmic landscapes of Breughel, the camp buildings were transformed by his pen into magnificent ruins, the people he portrayed inhabited the same earth, warmed themselves by the same sun, loved, yearned and died as always and everywhere – in the nightmares of Bosch, the phantasmagoria of Goya, the pastorals of Watteau. And into this timeless land the artist escaped from the present, in which he had not the strength to live. Under such conditions artistic endeavour had no practical purpose. There was not even the hope that one day these drawings might gain their freedom and become the property of others. Under such conditions artistic endeavour was transformed from a professional activity into a form of existence, the creation of a private world in which to live and preserve oneself as a human being. In this way art acquired an intensity, sharpness and relevance such that it rarely possesses. It is possible that had Sveshnikov not painted he would not have survived.

The case of Sveshnikov is not an exception, but common enough among artists now working in the Soviet Union. Wherever the artist paints – in his room, studio or camp hut – he creates a world of his own beyond the confines of which – and this, surely, is the essential experience of the intelligentsia in contemporary Russia – there is a void where only permitted paintings, authorised books, sanctioned plays and approved symphonies can exist. Such works do not perpetuate cultural traditions (they do not even seek to replace them with new values); they simply carry out the latest party directives. So when, after the death of Stalin, the threat of immediate transfer from studio to prison cell for disagreement with these directives had lessened, artists began fervently to create (and the public fervently to consume) the phenomenon, which subsequently became known by the name of Soviet unofficial art. They eagerly visited the foreign exhibitions and devoured books, journals and reproductions. Old Russian icon-painting, foreign classics, the art of the Soviet avant-garde of the 1920s, contemporary western painting – all of which for decades had been carefully concealed, turned out to be fundamentally different from anything they had been taught at the institutes of education. Rather than have the right to call themselves members of the Union of Soviet Artists and to enjoy the accompanying privileges, they preferred to be citizens of world culture. They worked as labourers, hospital orderlies, nightwatchmen, while at home in their boxrooms, basements and attics they painted whatever their hearts and talents dictated, in the manner that the great models of past and present art had taught them. Having embarked on this path, they automatically excluded themselves from official artistic life. Not because their art was politically tendentious, anti-social or non-realistic, but because it had changed, as it were, its citizenship.

And so, sitting in their rooms, studios or cells, with the sense of being in a cultural void, Soviet artists paint . . . But what? Here we return to our point of departure – the misunderstanding which occurs whenever the Russian avant-garde comes into contact with contemporary western culture.

I used to find it somewhat bizarre to see an artist, in some Moscow basement, composing arrangements in the spirit of American pop art, or covering his canvas with conceptual formulae. It was as if a tailor were sewing buttons on to a suit, which had not yet been cut. On the other hand, this same process outside Russia is seen as something quite natural. This is because in the West the material of reality has already been cut up, sewn together and reshaped a thousand times by the mechanism of culture, it has undergone aesthetic processing in the various cultural spheres – in literature, the cinema, television etc., so that now, perhaps, the artist's lot is restricted to the invention of new forms and creative concepts. The situation is very different in Russia, where reality – all that has happened here over the past decades and is happening now – remains outside the sphere of cultural processing, unable to find its reflection and interpretation in art. Thus every genuine artist working here takes upon himself the role of interpreter of this still uninterpreted reality – without even the risk of repeating what has been done before him.

Whereas artists in Russia work in a cultural vacuum, western artists live in a climate of cultural inflation (too many values are created, they are too easily accessible and therefore they depreciate). Perhaps this is the basic reason why the nonconformism of the western avant-garde is permeated with a spirit of the rejection of all established structures, including the aesthetic. Its representatives call themselves the left wing in art, and often their aesthetic leftishness coincides with their political views. The nonconformist artists of the Soviet Union are also referred to as 'left-wing', but – and here is yet another Russian paradox – their creative activity is by no means determined by a spirit of struggle or protest, nor by the rejection of past cultural values. They are rather the guardians of these values and therefore, from the point of view of the West, they belong more to the right, than to left-wing artistic ideology (it is no coincidence that the iconoclastic zeal of Ernst Neizvestny is

closer to many here, than Boris Sveshnikov's deep spiritualism,
I. Kabakov's search for new artistic concepts, or Boris Birger's
attempts to enrich traditional means of expression).

All these misleading paradoxes serve only to prove that
political terminology (right–left, progressive–conservative etc.)
works no better when applied to art than, for example, in
anatomy, where the left leg in no way contradicts the right and
can scarcely claim to be the more progressive. On the roads of
art it is not the stated destinations which are important, but the
natural and organic nature of the processes.

The organic nature of the processes taking place in unofficial
Soviet art is determined by the phenomena described above.
Within the cultural vacuum they inherit, artists in Russia are
striving to restore the broken links of cultural continuity:
behind their creative search there is always a sense of nostalgia
for the lost culture which still lies buried somewhere in man's
soul. Thus we find in the works of Sveshnikov images of the
past which ring out like familiar melodies amid the cacophony
of twentieth-century art. In the style of his drawings we can
sense the Gothic brittleness of a Dürer engraving, the dry,
precision of the old Flemish masters, or the elegant line of
rococo. In the tachist landscapes of Zverev the seething colour-
fulness of nineteenth-century romanticism may suddenly burst
forth. The drawings of Plavinsky occasionally weave the
whimsical patterns characteristic of Old Russian script. The
fantastic world of Kharitonov lives by the aesthetic laws of
former times, and the manner in which the paint is applied to
his canvas is sometimes reminiscent of the disintegrating
texture of an old fresco. Rabin, in his urban landscapes,
prefers winding Moscow alleys designed for people to broad
thoroughfares built for cars and parades; he prefers shop signs
to slogans and brick belfries to breeze-block monstrosities. All
these artists seem to be building bridges from the present
moment to the eternal, from transient, social problems to
universal, existential values. If this art needs defining, then I
would define it as art which is graphic in form and nostalgic in
content.

This cultural nostalgia does not necessarily imply social
criticism or protest. This art summons no one, leads nowhere
in particular, nor does it seek to overthrow. It is defined in the

first place not by searchings in the field of pure form, but by traditionalism within the broad spectrum of all Russian and world culture. And here the question arises which so many western observers have sought in vain to answer. Why, in that case, is this art underground? Why are these works piled up behind wardrobes and under beds, hidden from the gaze of outsiders, instead of setting a shining example at official Soviet exhibitions? A concrete example will perhaps help solve this riddle.

Boris Birger* spent the whole war at the front. After demobilisation he graduated from the Moscow Surikov Institute of Art and began to take part in exhibitions from 1953. His early works were in the spirit of the 'Knave of Diamonds' and other 'left-wing trends' of the 1920s. He experimented with colour and form, introducing into the musty atmosphere of the post-Stalin period a fresh breeze of creativity and innovation. Soon he achieved fame and the Soviet press began to refer to him as 'one of the leading young artists'. It was not, however, until Birger reached a mature age that he found his own path in art. The search for new forms was replaced by a desire to consolidate his own artistic vision and to develop a technique of painting for its embodiment. He turned to the Rembrandtesque tradition of light and shade, employing a complex method of multi-coloured brush strokes, whereby every millimetre of canvas is composed of several pigments. His style evolved from conventionalism to realism (in this respect he is close to R. Falk), and now among the Moscow artists one could hardly name a more subtle painter of portraits or an artist who was better able to express the inner life of things. But as soon as Birger achieved a level surpassing Soviet aesthetic standards, he was accused of formalism, expelled from the Moscow Branch of the Artists Union and denied the chance to hold exhibitions.

Such is the fate of many Russian artists. As early as 1919, writing in *Proletarian Art*, the talented critic Nikolai Punin, who perished in Stalin's camps, wrote: 'The realists are talentless not as individuals, but as a school, as a form of art. The reason why there are no gifted artists among the realists is not that a chance period of stagnation has overtaken the school,

* There are few works by Birger in the West, and it was not possible to bring them together for the Grenoble exhibition.

but because all that is talented flees from the school, just as life itself flees from yesterday towards tomorrow.' Now, fifty years later, this statement by Punin can be applied with even greater justification to Socialist Realism, which arose in the conditions of the Stalin regime, died together with it, but is now being resurrected by its apologists. The output of its representatives was produced at a time of sharp decline in artistic standards. They spent the last grains of their talent and professional skill in fulfilling official orders, yet they continue to this day to occupy the leading positions in Soviet art. It is enough to mention that the president of the Academy of Arts of the USSR is now the sculptor Tomsky – once Stalin's court portraitist, who in his day inundated the country with thousands of statues of his master. Like the characters in Kafka who spend their lives in attics, these artists can exist only in the stuffy atmosphere of cultural vacuum; the slightest breath of fresh air from the outside world of culture is fatal to them. Therefore the struggle between official and unofficial art in the USSR is not a clash of two different political ideologies. It is the struggle of anti-culture – Socialist Realism may be called an anti-culture in the precise, scientific meaning of the word, for it has lived not by the creation of something new, but by the destruction of former values – against culture. It is the conflict of all that is talentless, inert and servile with the talented, new and sincere. Today, at official Soviet exhibitions, one can sometimes see bad 'formalism', but it is almost impossible to meet talented art, even of the realist kind.

That was the last and, for Soviet artists, perhaps the most painful paradox of all, one which has sprung from the soil of the total surrealism of Soviet reality over the past few decades.

The Literary Process in Russia

ABRAM TERZ
(Andrei Sinyavsky)

> 'It has reached a point where in the craft of literature
> I value only proud flesh, only rogue tumours:
>> "The whole ravine is stricken to the bone
>> By the falcon's piercing shriek . . ."
> I divide all works of literature throughout the world
> into those permitted and those written without
> permission. The first are so much garbage; the
> second sort are stolen air. I want to spit in the faces
> of those writers who write with prior approval; I
> want to beat them about the head with a stick and
> sit them all down at a table in the Herzen House,
> having placed in front of each one a glass of police
> tea and given each of them an analysis of Gornfeld's
> urine.'
>
> OSIP MANDELSTAM *'Fourth Prose'*

'The writer writes when he feels like it, the reader reads when he has nothing better to do . . .' This tradition, which arose in what for the art of literature was the relatively peaceful nineteenth century, has been broken in our present age. The Russian author who does not want to write to the state's direction has assumed the nightmarish status of an underground writer, that is to say, from the state's point of view he has chosen a life of crime, for which strict penalties and deterrents are laid down. Literature has become a forbidden, risky, and thus all the more fascinating activity.

Imagine the situation described by Anatoly Kuznetsov,*

---

* Soviet writer, born in 1929, author of *Babi Yar* and other novels. In 1967 he defected while on a visit to the West and now lives in England.

quoted indignantly in *Literary Gazette** from Kuznetsov's own words, in which he told how he spent his solitary leisure time until he left Russia. Having, it seems, composed several mysterious manuscripts, this writer sealed them in glass preserving jars and buried them in his garden one dark night. He was, as the saying goes, covering his traces, burying his ill-gotten gains, just as thieves and robbers everywhere have always done. 'What sort of writer can he be *after this*?' demanded *Literary Gazette* indignantly, naïvely unaware that this whole scene, which could have come out of *Treasure Island*, is a splendid one; that it not only excites children and the rising generation, always ready to follow a romantic example; but that a writer's heart, above all, is gladdened by an episode of this kind because it strikes a chord on certain hidden strings in his innermost nature. Even the authorities call us 'artists of the written word'; so it is not our business to sit on the presidium, nor to run around panting after workmen on the site of the Bratsk hydro-electric station, creating a set of tactless, phoney, hail-fellow-well-met relationships between those workers, the heroes of our books and our readers. Because in the end we are neither merchants, nor salesmen, nor political leaders, and even titles like 'professor' or 'academician' sound too positive. The first and favourite part of a writer's job is simply that: to bury jars in the ground, jars with manuscripts, and in those manuscripts . . . aha! wouldn't you like to know what's in those manuscripts!

For Anatoly Kuznetsov to have reached the decision on his own initiative to seal up those fruit-preserving jars, society, art and literature had to proceed for a long time up a blind alley (which is, in the end, most likely to offer the best way out). The writer had to be reduced to the status of a criminal, a law-breaker – to which end some writers first had to be driven to suicide, others expelled, still others tortured. Thousands of writers had to be corrupted and castrated – a task undertaken for several decades by the founders and stormy petrels† of

---

* The leading Moscow literary weekly.
† This is an oblique derogatory reference to Maxim Gorky. In his pre-revolutionary writings Gorky often used the pseudonym of 'the stormy petrel'. After the Revolution, particularly in the late 20s and 30s, Stalin exploited Gorky's world-wide prestige to bring Russian writers to a state of subservience.

Soviet literature. The guardians of Soviet literary orthodoxy are now offended because, they complain, Anatoly Kuznetsov, like some thief, sets about burying his precious jars in the garden of his dacha by night . . .

Thus at a certain stage the literary process has assumed the character of a double-edged game, an escapade which in itself could well provide the plot of an entertaining novel. Authors have been turned into the heroes of as yet unwritten books; they have tasted the savour of an intrigue which may end in disaster ('If you play with fire, you can burn your fingers,' as Khrushchev warned writers with his customary bluntness), but which on the other hand lends a certain higher meaning – a gaiety, an interest, 'a pledge, who knows, of immortality' – to the writer's otherwise drab existence. All this has given to Russian literature a shock, a stimulus to its development, and now, as at no other time since its 'de-kulakisation' it is full of strength and hope for the future. At this moment the fate of the Russian writer has become the most intriguing, the most fruitful literary topic in the whole world: he is either being imprisoned, pilloried, internally exiled or simply kicked out. The writer nowadays is walking a knife-edge; but unlike the old days, when writers were simply eliminated one after another, he now derives pleasure and moral satisfaction from this curious pastime. The writer is now someone to be reckoned with. And all the attempts to make him see reason, to terrorise or crush him, to corrupt or liquidate him, only raise his literary achievement to higher and higher levels.

Fortunately our bosses in Russia, even those who have two university degrees and know three foreign languages, by some innate tendency remain profoundly and hopelessly uneducated people. They persist in believing that they can regulate the artistic process and direct it into legitimate channels by using various forms of coercion. They believe that they only have to say: 'Clap him in jail!' for a writer to turn out an epic poem of genius in praise of communism triumphant. They are also, to our good fortune, ignorant of history. They take no account of Oscar Wilde, who, though he was not imprisoned for his writings, still moves the world to tears by the trauma he suffered as a writer and by the *Ballad of Reading Gaol*. They forget Dante, who was not exiled from his native city for being a good poet, but whose fate has nevertheless made the words 'Dante', 'exile' and 'writer' into virtual synonyms. Nor was Pushkin killed because he was a writer. . . . But if they did kill a writer because he was a writer, imagine what a twist in the plot of history that writer's adventures would acquire, when the powers that be were prepared, in the final analysis, to do him to death . . . !

The time has now come to pity not the writers but their persecutors and oppressors, for it is to them that Russian literature owes its success. And what of the writer? He has no worries; there he is, sitting calmly in prison or in the madhouse, hugging himself with delight: a story! And as he breathes his last, he can rub his hands: the job's done!

The best place to observe the new boom in Russian literature is the customs house. What do they search for more than anything else? Manuscripts. Not gold, not diamonds, not even the plan of a Soviet factory, but – manuscripts! And what do they most search for when you enter Russia? Books. Books in Russian. In other words, Russian literature, as it passes back and forth, has a value. Therefore a dike, a dam, the size of the Bratsk dam, must be erected to ensure that no books or manuscripts can penetrate it. Yet even so they seep through.

When they discovered that a woman of my acquaintance, going to Russia from the West, was carrying a copy of *Doctor Zhivago* in her suitcase, she was immediately put into a gynaecological chair and subjected to a medical examination to find out whether she might be carrying any more banned novels. This is excellent. This is all to the good. It means that a book is worth something, it is sought after, pursued; and by escaping, hiding, or being buried in the ground it gathers weight and power. Nowadays it is not dollars but manuscripts that are quoted on the market.

Now let us examine the subject matter of most of these manuscripts. We shall not be far wrong if we say that the major topics are prison and labour camps. The themes which inspire the Russian writer today are not stories about collective farms, or factories, not love stories nor even the pangs of youth, but how people are imprisoned, where they are sent into exile and exactly how (interesting topic, you must admit) they shoot you in the back of the neck. The labour camp is now the central, the dominant theme of literature. In a short space of time we have succeeded by stealth, by quietly burrowing away, in composing a hitherto unique, unheard of series of novels, stories, poems and memoirs around the motif of penal servitude. Dostoyevsky's 'Notes from the House of the Dead' is *vieux jeu*; all Russia is now howling about the House of the Dead through the megaphone of literature.

Ultimately all these books, complete with scholarly commentaries, are published in the West; yet as soon as it catches the sound of that wolfish howl, the West's reaction is naturally one of baffled amazement:

'For all those years you Russians were silent, you endured uncomplainingly and even glorified the régime; yet now, *now* — when *practically no one* is being imprisoned, you start reading the burial service over the régime and hinder us from trading with it! How many dissidents are there, anyway, in your multi-million population? You can count them on the fingers of one hand. And isn't there a limit to what can be written on a single topic?'

To which I would reply:

'Go ahead, dear friends, trade to your hearts' content; but when you sup with the Devil, remember to use a long spoon.'

Apart, of course, from the effect of old wounds, I am certain that there is now a literary law at work, in obedience to which Russian writers have fallen in love with their own unfreedom. We wouldn't give it up now for all the tea in China. We'd sooner die of starvation than stop writing about the bullet in the back of the neck. There's nothing for it: the plot has to end with a firing squad.

What did you imagine? Did you think you could crush people with tanks without some maverick or dissident then using your tanks in his novel? Did you not realise that the voices of the dead would one day be heard out of the mouths of the half-dead? You killed Babel, you killed Tsvetaeva, you killed Mandelstam* — yet you still imagine all that will leave no trace in Russian literature? Don't fool yourselves. You'd better go and read some history. Somewhere way back in the seventeenth century, some useless archpriest called Avvakum† was flung into

---

* Osip Mandelstam, born in 1891, a leading early Soviet poet, was arrested for the first time in 1934. He died in prison in 1938.
† A Russian priest, born in 1620, famous for his schismatic rebellion against the Orthodox Patriarch and for his autobiography.

a pit. And what he wrote in his underground prison still filters through to us to this day, which ought to be enough to make you think.

One day a Soviet official – the episode took place in a prison camp – summoned an orphan juvenile delinquent to a character-building pep talk; the lad, who came from the fringe of the underworld, had managed to pick up some scraps of education in his wanderings between various camps and transit prisons and had begun to make sense of it. For fifty years, the official said, our enemies have thought we were rotting away, but we have done nothing but grow bigger and stronger. So, he said, you'd better not get mixed up in that pointless business, and you might as well make due apology to the powers that be.

'But,' replied the young miscreant, 'the Roman Empire lasted even longer, yet even so it collapsed in the end.'

'What? The Roman Empire? But that . . . that's *history*! (a sigh of relief) I'm talking to you about what's happening today, so why do you bring up history?'

In other words, as far as that official was concerned neither our heroic modern age nor himself and his fortress had the slightest connection with *history* – an instance of the benefit we derive from having such uneducated, or semi-educated leaders. History is not their department; so if anyone makes references to Avvakum or Dante, there's no need to worry: they won't help anyone or teach any lessons – they're just history.

In a similar heart-to-heart chat, another official – this time outside the prison walls – for lack of any better argument, gave himself away by saying quietly: 'We ought to crush you with tanks! With tanks I say!' Once again, the poor fellow had forgotton that the effect of tanks is simply to produce, as though by conveyer belt, yet another upsurge of manuscripts and books in incalculable numbers. Somehow the bosses can't help bungling things when they deal with Russian literature. They expel someone from the Union of Writers and announce with glee: 'He's not a writer – he's simply a criminal!' And yet this verdict is balm to the soul of the expelled writer: at last he's made it!

But enough of fun and games; let us proceed to the theoretical aspect. The quotation from Mandelstam, which heads this article in the form of an epigraph, proclaims that all true writing – even when no clash with authority is involved – is something forbidden, something reprehensible, and in this illicit element lies the whole excitement, the whole dilemma of being a writer. Take any great work of literature: it is either an explosion or a freak. ('All you writers should be put in the madhouse!' my cell-mate in the Lubyanka – an informer – once said to me frankly, and in some higher, metaphysical sense he was right.) Whether we take Pushkin's *Eugene Onegin*, or for greater respectablity Tolstoy's *Resurrection*, we will notice that both of them are based on the notion of escape, of breaking the bounds; that the writer's very soul longs to escape; that the savour, the sense, the ideal of being a writer is nothing whatever to do with 'telling the truth' (go and tell it if you want to – in a tramcar), but is to do with planting that so-called 'truth' across the tracks of the 'lie' which is universally, legally and publicly accepted as truth – and thus to assume, as a duty, the role of 'criminal', 'law-breaker', 'renegade', 'degenerate', or (what an apt new word they have invented!) an 'ideological saboteur'. Every self-respecting writer of any significance is a saboteur (hell – no dynamite!) and as he surveys the horizon wandering what to write about, more often than not he will choose some forbidden topic, be it the labour camp, prison, the Jews, the KGB or (what else is there that's forbidden?) – sex. That is why I insist that freedom of speech, of all things, is bad for a writer; that freedom can cause a writer to wilt and fade, like a flower in too strong sunlight. Good for a writer are darkness, prison camp, the lash, the gag and the ban (though at the same time with the chance, for those who are bold enough, of wrenching away that gag or evading the law). Deep in his gut, the writer longs not for freedom but for *liberation*, as someone who understands that mechanism once said. The very act of writing is a liberation (give me my chains!). The point is to open a valve, and for that to be done the valve must first of all be pretty firmly shut. And so, the tighter the noose is pulled around the writer's neck (within certain limits, of course), the better and more cheerfully, on the whole, will he sing his song.

The language of literature, if one takes a close look at it, is the language of obscenity. In a broad sense, the language of literature is a string of four-letter words – even when the writer uses it to say: 'How lovely, how fresh the roses were!' You think he means roses? You're wrong; those words are a curse, which the writer (in this case Turgenev) is hurling at the walls of a prison. In the family circle or among friends it would be improper to talk in the way a writer writes. The literary language is a breakaway from language; it is the language of frank statements that would make ordinary people ashamed or horrified, the language of direct confrontation with reality on ultimate issues, when you say to it (reality): 'Come along with me, or I'll murder you!' And then you say to it with feeling: 'How lovely, how fresh the roses were!' (In other words – 'Come along with me, or I'll murder you!') Reality, of course, does not believe in the writer and replies: We know your sort! But it doesn't know *that* sort. And if it refuses to go with him (it usually doesn't go with the writer; he's a rogue . . .) but stays with more dignified, practical people like generals and engineers, then the writer, in reproach, hurls his usual obscenity at it: 'How lovely,' he says, 'how fresh the roses were!'

I chose the most decent example, but if I were to take Pushkin or Lermontov instead, then you would have to stop your ears.

The writer is an attempt to carry on a conversation with people about the things that are most vital and most dangerous. The writer is the Morse code tapped out by drowning men in a submarine. To spend all his life drowning and trying to make himself understood in groans and curses: that is the writer's lot. All those novels with titles like *For Whom the Bell Tolls* or *Each Man Dies Alone* are tolling for no one but the author, the writer. So you can sleep in peace.

The writer is an extreme, blood-stained appeal made by man to man. How and in what way they talk in such cases doesn't matter very much. They are saying – and that is obvious from the start if you are a writer, as soon as you pick up your pen – things that are forbidden, and nothing else. Otherwise, why write? Why not just use the polite, commonplace language used in the tramcar?

The writer is the last, knowingly doomed attempt at a bombing raid: his is the ability to appeal ceaselessly to truth and justice without the slightest hope of ever attaining them. And if some fine author should say to you tomorrow: 'I've broken through! Eureka! Follow me!' you may not believe him, but follow him all the same, because he knows what he's doing; he has been able to break the ban and will utter, with his last breath, an unknown word of liberation.

In fact it has never been vouchsafed to anyone, except to saints, to come within hailing distance of the truth, and when the writer speaks his beautiful words, he is simply dying. Surely you can hear that the writer is in his death-agony as he speaks?

I am amazed that society still tolerates, acknowledges and even extols the writer. The writer is a living corpse, the shadow of a man; he is a man who has taken up his cross. What are stylistic skill and literary form? What form? The form of a coffin? That is why I cannot understand Chekhov, who advised that all aspirant writers should be whipped, while being told: 'Don't write! Don't write!' You might just as well beat people and animals while telling them: 'Don't die!'

The experienced, hard-bitten writer should not just be whipped: he should be flung out of decent society. Yet he is honoured, congratulated when he finishes his current novel. He is paid money. Quite honestly, whenever I earn any money – and I earn it regularly from my literary works – I am amazed every time it happens and I carry the money away in haste, clutching my pocket, crouching slightly like a burglar removing the silver cutlery from the scene of the theft.

It is time, however, to go back to Russia, to the more concrete and more immediate matter of banned literature, for which people are paid no money but to make up for it they are well and truly punished. We would sit in the prison camp and laugh as we read occasional copies of *Literary Gazette*, which periodically informed us that yet another writer had defected or despatched his pernicious manuscript by illegal means across the frontier, or that the imperialists had published and made use of some stolen manuscript. It mentioned Arkady Belinkov, Voinovich, Serebryakova, Tvardovsky, Svetlana Alliluyeva, Kuznetsov* and so on, until this list of those labouring to create an uncensored Russian literature was crowned by N. S. Khrushchev (who not long ago had been spitting at Falck's

* Modern Soviet writers who all had their work taken abroad and published there.

canvases*), who in his old age had also gone to the bad and by some incredible means had published his memoirs in the West. It seemed that at any moment all our official luminaries, including Fedin, Mikhalkov†, and the present members of the government might personally take part – keeping it secret from each other – in the parallel literary process, which no threats seem able to stop.

Bad examples are contagious. In addition, the state of unfreedom – not as total as it was under Stalin, but still a lack of freedom oppressive enough to stimulate the urge to kick over the traces and write – has hastened the process. Over the short period of my prison-camp sentence (I did not personally observe this happening at close quarters), there appeared in Russia a body of writing which, while not yet the first in literary quality, was at any rate the most interesting in the world: an *alternative* to the officially sanctioned, published literature. As ever, the decorous, censored, printed literature, rewarded with dachas and trips abroad to meet writers from Asia and Africa, has not been sparklingly original and has ended up in a style resembling some sort of deadly automatic writing. The alternative literature called itself simply and modestly 'Samizdat'.‡ It has been our privilege to live to see a *second* literature.

It would be hard to invent a more precise and more inoffensive name than 'Samizdat', indicating no more than that a person has simply written everything he wanted to say as he thought fit, and has published it himself, regardless of the consequences, by passing a wad of typewritten sheets to a friend. That friend has gone running to boast about it to two more like-minded drop-outs – and we are witnessing the conception of something great, fantastic, unique, incomparable: the embryo of Russian literature, which once before, in the nineteenth century, delighted mankind, and is now once more feeling the urge to return to the old battleground.

* This refers to Nikita Khrushchev's appearance at an Art Exhibition in Moscow's Manezh Hall in 1963, when he made extremely coarse remarks about some of the modernistic paintings.
† Konstantin Fedin and Sergei Mikhalkov were two of the most conformist Soviet writers.
‡ This acronym means literally 'self-publishing'. It is the reproduction, usually on a typewriter with many carbon copies, of a banned or unpublishable literary work.

Apart from new and unknown authors (unknown even to the State Security forces), in the first, dawning stage of 'Samizdat' the manuscript copies included names like Tsvetaeva, Mandelstam, Pasternak, Akhmatova,* and that was enough to give this new publishing venture the best possible recommendation. (Ideally, in principle, there is not and cannot be anything sweeter to the writer's ear than 'Samizdat', 'self-publication'.) We shall never understand the history of the most recent 'Samizdat' (in a broad sense) literature if we forget that the greatest poets of the twentieth century stood at its cradle; if while pinning our hopes on the future of Russian [samizdat] writers, we do not in the first instance do honour to those four, of whom the first committed suicide, the second perished in a prison camp, and the luckiest, who lived to old age, turned out to be Akhmatova and Pasternak. It was Pasternak who, in his declining days – when the authorities, to the accompaniment of much phoney indignation, were planning to expel him from Russia – carried a phial of poison in his pocket in order, if need be, to complete the long list of Soviet poets who committed suicide. And it was Akhmatova (another lucky one) who wrote about the civil execution to which she was subjected in the memorable year of 1946:†

> Like a wounded beast you have
> Hoisted me up on a bloodstained hook –
> That foreigners, *exulting, wondering* and *not believing*
> Might circle round and gaze at me . . .‡

That terrible string of present participles . . .

To this day Anna Akhmatova's *Requiem* circulates in Russia only in manuscript copies (it's safe – just verses from someone's private album). Shortly before his death, when Pasternak learned of the appearance of the illegal little manuscript journal *Sintaxis* (its publisher, Alek Ginzburg, was arrested

---

* Boris Pasternak (1890–1960), famous mainly for his translations of Shakespeare and for his novel *Dr Zhivago*, was subjected to an official campaign of abuse in 1958 when he was awarded the Nobel Prize for Literature. Anna Akhmatova (1889–1966), an important Russian poet before and after the Revolution, suffered a similar campaign in 1946.
† The word 'execution' is used metaphorically.
‡ Quoted from memory, from Akhmatova's own words. *Author.*

after the fourth issue), made up entirely of youthful verse, he lamented bitterly that he could not join the ranks of these embryonic writers by appearing in their home-made student magazines. That was the dawn of 'Samizdat'; that was the thread of life which linked the future of Russian literature with its heroic past.

At the beginning of the twentieth century we had the most beautiful poetry in the world. I am certain that in those days no other people had such poetry; but prose, as we know, develops later, and it was blighted by the frost. We have not attained the flowering of Russian prose in our century. However, the awareness that around the beginning of this century Russia was fortunate enough to experience an age of sublime poetry; that by some miracle these poems have survived to our day and have now become our contemporaries – this awareness has committed Russian prose literature to strain every nerve to prove that it, too, can achieve greatness. The poetry of the early part of the century means that at least towards the end of the century the prose that has hitherto been lacking *must* appear. If it appears (and it is beginning to appear), then our eternal gratitude is due to those poets, who were able at the very start to inform Russian literature with such a sweep and such an electric charge that it has been able to leap across the gaping chasm of thirty or forty years, in which Russian literature virtually did not exist and in which, worst of all, there was no certainty that it ever would exist again.

In a historical perspective of the literary process in Russia, that period which for convenience we have marked with the searing brand of 'Stalinism', has also, perhaps, made its modest but legitimate contribution to this process. It may be that too long a spell of silence and despair has made us speak up with such passion and fervour in the conditions of today's relatively tolerable (and even, as I have said, in some ways beneficial) unfreedom – in other words, as soon as the writers were able so much as to open their mouths. If nowadays we shout so loudly to the world at large about the terrible and shameful things that are being done in Russia, then it is because, among other things, we have had direct experience of the 'cold and murk of days to come' which Alexander Blok prophesied for us all. Of course, some of the most worthwhile authors were working in the Stalinist era, at least until they were finished off. But at the time Russia did not know that there were writers alive and writing on the most important, forbidden themes and in equally forbidden language. Only now has the voice of Mandelstam reached us from his exile in remote Voronezh. Only thirty years afterwards, like some underwater spectre, some man drowned in that epoch, did Bulgakov's* novel *The Master and Margarita* float to the surface: an example of the advantage of concealing manuscripts in good time, manuscripts which 'do not burn' only because they are buried deep – under the ground, under water.

I shall allow myself to dwell a little on that novel, taking it at one, and perhaps not the most serious, of its levels – namely that of the author's autobiography, the element which concerns Bulgakov's personal fate. The night in which the novel was written was of such unrelieved darkness that only the devil himself inspired even the faintest trust. The role of the devil, the dark genius, the role of Woland, who for certain mysterious, incomprehensible reasons treats the writer – the Master – with indulgence, was played in Bulgakov's own life by – Stalin. Stalin knew about Bulgakov, and having driven him into a corner, gave orders, for some reason, that he was not to be touched. Although he granted him no privileges, he nevertheless allowed Bulgakov's seditious play to be performed at the Moscow Arts Theatre – the one theatre in the country where it was permitted (in general Stalin had a weakness for the singular number); Stalin himself went there to see that play, *The Days of the Turbins*,† secretly and regularly (I almost said 'at night'). Although the link was as thin as a telephone wire, Stalin even maintained personal contact with Bulgakov. By all the standards of the time, the author of *The Master and Margarita* should have been shot, and it is very likely that had Stalin suspected the existence of that novel, Bulgakov would have been killed, the manuscript burnt and its ashes scattered to the winds. Yet instead, other writers were arrested and shot, including the most 'proletarian', the most importunate in their devotion to

---

* Mikhail Bulgakov (1881–1940), a well-known Soviet novelist and playwright.
† A play based on Bulgakov's novel *The White Guard*, performed in Moscow in 1926.

the Party, such as Averbakh;* *The Master and Margarita*
contains descriptions of the Sodom, the Bedlam of the literary
establishment of the time, which for a long time had howled
for Bulgakov's blood, having pilloried him all over the country
as a White Guardist who had escaped the firing-squad, an
establishment which itself now suddenly perished in a manner
far worse than the fate of the White Guard. Bulgakov, on the
other hand, survived by an inscrutable irony of fate; driven
into a corner, he described in the novel his strange friendship
with Woland,† who, having contrived and deployed every
form of sorcery, turned out to be morally far superior to the
human beings he chastised. Men became devils, and the chief
devil became a Maecenas. The only people helped by Woland,
being a master of evil, were the Master and his Margarita (she
it was, in real life, who saved and preserved the manuscript
of the novel), because Woland knew 'who' was 'who'. This
mystery of their relationship, between writer and political
leader (as in the underworld proverb describing the attitude
of a powerful gang boss to some distinguished non-criminal
figure: 'I'm big – you're big'), was even reflected in the
graphic proximity of their names, in which the initial 'W' of
*W*oland is the reversed monogram of the *M*aster and *M*argarita.

> He believes in the mutual comprehension
> Of two opposing principles, as far apart
> as things can be . . .

as Pasternak wrote at the same period on the similarly mystical
theme of the relationship between Poet and Leader (in concrete terms, the relationship between Pasternak and Stalin).

Yes, Stalin could inspire not only horror and love, but also
faith in his magic powers. In particular among the theosophists,
despite the fact that they were persecuted and had no great
love for the régime, a legend was in circulation to the effect that
Stalin knew something which no one else could ever discover
and that he was an incarnation of Manu, the Great Teacher of
India. On the historical plane, however, Bulgakov's fascination
with Woland has far more justification, for in this personifi-

---

* A minor writer, well known for his harsh attack on 'bourgeois'
writers under Stalin.
† An all powerful, devil-like creature, the 'Master' of Bulgakov's novel.

cation Stalin appears as an amazing conjuror, unique in his profession (hence his fellow feeling in the novel for the masterly professional writer – Bulgakov), who devoted himself totally to the art of confusing and making fools of people, conjuring up every possible kind of mirage and hallucination. In Stalin, with his firing-squads and show trials, his cunning and sorcery, his ability to stand above the rest of humanity, and in the grim solitude of an evil, omniscient and all-powerful spirit, Bulgakov no doubt sensed an artistic streak and exaggerated it in his fantasies about Woland.

Of course neither Woland nor Bulgakov's novel as a whole add up to a picture of Stalin, just as the book does not constitute the author's autobiography. But through it we can gain a better understanding of the specific way in which art developed in our country, which at a certain moment was *totally* replaced by the games played by a single Magician, who for a lengthy period was able to lend to history itself the power and the appearance of fairy-tale fantasy. Art vanished and rotted away so that for a while life (if one looks at it from a standpoint that is detached and tolerant of evil) might acquire the aesthetic savour of bloody, nightmarish farce, played out according to theatrical and literary rules. One only has to take, for example, the detective-novel conception of history which the Leader managed to inculcate into millions of people, or his love of turning metaphors into reality. Metaphorical turns of phrase such as: 'lackeys of imperialism', 'traitors to the working class', 'hirelings of capital', 'left-wing bias', 'right-wing deviation' and so on, which were widely current well before Stalin took over and which, largely used for intra-party abuse, were even provided with a *scientific* foundation – without intending any reference to their literal meaning, i.e. that a 'lackey' is someone who stands beside a bourgeois table holding a tray, and a 'hireling' is someone who soils dollar bills with his grubby fingers – Stalin, I repeat, brought these metaphors to complete, flesh-and-blood life. The tragic pathos of 1937 lay not only in the extent to which the country was gripped by a kind of Bacchic orgy, nor in the fact that the purge went so far as to destroy the most loyal of party zealots, but also in the extraordinarily vivid way, as though in a novel, in which metaphors were given life – when the whole country was suddenly crawling with all kinds of invisible (and therefore specially dangerous) reptiles, snakes and scorpions with terrible names such as 'Trotskyite' or 'wrecker'. Stalin probably wanted simply to instil in people a feeling of disgust for the political rivals that he was destroying everywhere and for suspect persons in general, so that people should not feel pain at killing their fathers and brothers of yesterday. But what happened was that Russia became filled with 'enemies', no less literal for being invisible, who acted like devils and blurred the line between reality and fantasy. Stalin had brought into play (possibly without suspecting it) the magic powers contained in the language, and Russian society, ever susceptible to a graphic perception of words and to the miraculous transformation of life into the plot of a novel (the source, incidentally, of the beauty and grandeur of Russian literature), submitted to the terrifying illusion of living in a world of miracles, sorcery, perfidy and artifice. These were visibly in control of reality and, as they sent shivers down everyone's spine, they produced a certain intense, theatrical pleasure. Naturally there were innocent, sincere people like young Pavlik Morozov,* longing with all the ardour of their guiltless, childish hearts to denounce their own fathers for the sake of 'truth' and 'for the good of the cause'. And there were wives who informed on their husbands, not because they were coerced into it but for conscience's sake; for the blood of the victims of the firing-squads, as it drenched the country, seemed to be the blood of the people being sucked by those vampire-like enemies – enemies who should be mercilessly destroyed, as befits vampires. A wasp sting in your coffins, you enemies the people!

From that legendary, fiction-dominated epoch we have retained to this day the habit of believing in the power of words. When we, for instance, pronounce such expressions as 'ideological saboteur', 'renegade', 'internal emigré' or 'dissimulator' (instead of the good old word 'double-dealer', unfortunately compromised by long use during the years of the cult of personality), or 'literary Vlasovite',† – we are seized by a double

---

* He was a young child who reported his parents to the Stalinist police for hoarding grain. They were arrested and he was killed by angry locals. He is now an official Soviet hero and martyr.
† Andrei Vlasov was a Soviet general who was taken prisoner in 1942 and then fought on the German side. The term 'Vlasovite' is now used by Soviet media as a synonym for 'traitor'.

sense of horror and loathing for anyone who has deserved that
sorry appellation. It would seem (according to logic) that an
'ideological saboteur' is something much milder and better
than an actual saboteur, who blows up bridges, sends a train
crashing down an embankment and drops strychnine into wells.
But no – it is worse, and much more harmful. 'Ideological'
(look at him squirming!) implies far more fanaticism, implies a
certain internal (as in 'internal emigré'), evasive force, rather
like the devil himself. This is no boy, who secretly gave his
friend a copy of *Doctor Zhivago* to read (and his friend informed
on him). We know these boys: 'It would have been better if
you had killed a man!' the investigators say to them. No, the
whole point is in the image of covert, underground activity
conjured up by the word.

One of my fellow inmates in prison camp was an old man who
had been sentenced to twenty-five years (he had already reached
the end of his term) for believing in God. He was an Orthodox
Christian, one of the 'Tikhonites',* i.e. one of those who do not
recognise the validity of the present, officially tolerated church
(to him, too, his interrogators had said: 'It would have been
better if you had killed a man!'). By today's standards (see the
Criminal Code of the RSFSR),† the maximum sentence he
could receive is seven years labour camp (for 'anti-Soviet
agitation and propaganda') or at the very most an extra five
years exile might have been added to the seven years. But the
old man had done twenty-five years in prison camps in accordance with the old, superseded code. The old man had already
withdrawn from life and had no wish to argue for his rights.
Several youngsters, however (some of those 'ideological
saboteurs' who were inside, and still are, for having read
Doctor Zhivago or something of the sort), used to write petitions
and complaints on the old man's behalf to the Procurator-
General, pointing out the obvious discrepancy between his
'crime' and its 'punishment'. And as far as I remember, the
answer that came from the Procurator-General – in our liberal
days of 'observing full legality' – was always the same:

* Tikhon was a Russian Orthodox priest who, in the early Soviet
years refused to obey the authority of the Patriarch and compromise
with the Soviet Government.
† The RSFSR is that large part of the Soviet Union which is known
generally as 'Russia'.

'No, he was correctly sentenced, because *in the guise of* religious agitation he was engaged in *anti-Soviet* propaganda!'

In other words, if the old man had openly engaged in anti-Soviet propaganda, he would have been sentenced to seven years as prescribed by law. But because he did it 'in the guise of . . .', then he can sweat out his full term of twenty-five years!

'In the guise of . . .' implies something much more horrible. Therefore a '*literary* Vlasovite' is much more dreadful than a 'Vlasovite' as such, even worse, perhaps, than General Vlasov himself. After all, Vlasov was simply a turncoat and traitor who defected to Hitler (a straightforward, comprehensible matter). But a 'literary' is someone crawling around among us, like some elusive ('ideological') creepy-crawly, and since this reptile is considerably more difficult to recognise and destroy (in such a way as to give no comfort to the West), in its artificial, 'literary' skin it can be put across as infinitely more detestable.

However hard the leaders of the régime may struggle to observe socialist legality, however often they may sign international 'Declarations of the Rights of Man' (it depends on which man!), they are in thrall to an emotional, artistic perception of words, no matter how legal or scientific those words may be. 'God, you damned writers,' they say, 'seem to think you can fool us – the way you go on about yumanism, litracher, iddyology and what not. This "yumanism" of yours is worse than the Tartar yoke, y'know. A yoke's a yoke (and we can bring it back if we have to), but all this stuff about "art" and "litracher" is a lot nastier, 'cos it's like a snake in the grass.'

Again I am inclined to feel sorry for those in authority. You cannot imagine what physical and mental pain is caused to them by what I call, with permission, the 'literary process'.

The Party boss walks up to the rostrum on the stage of history and reads from a piece of paper (he finds it difficult, too!) with a text prepared by his experts:

'Ladies and gents! . . .'

And all the ladies and gentlemen present (at least in Russia) laugh. Dimly recalling that, having gained two degrees and knowing three languages, he still has something to say and a point to make to this audience of damned 'interlekchuls', he thinks to himself: 'Ah, you creeps, just you put a foot wrong and it's the tanks for you!' And then with a great effort,

straining to pronounce the meaningless words, he speaks:
'The arts and ree-elity!'

Sweeping the members of the audience with a glum, black,
unblinking eye, he waggles his eyebrows to stop them laughing.
Sensing what is in the air, everyone falls silent and with serious
faces they listen to a report to the world at large on the new,
ever greater surge of artistic creativity in the USSR and on how
Soviet writers are penetrating ever more deeply into life. Meanwhile he is thinking: 'Penetrating into life indeed! They should
be doing it to a woman – from behind!' Then with more
eyebrow-play, and a deep sigh after drinking half a glass of
special Kremlin mineral water: 'We should crush you with
tanks! With tanks!'*

The Soviet leaders are, of course, a natural target for political
jokes. In recent times only the joke has kept that unique,
spontaneous vigour which is the hallmark of art and which
signifies something more than freedom of speech. However
much you suppress the joke (and there was time when telling
jokes could earn you a prison sentence of five or even ten years),
it only gathers strength from being suppressed – and not the
strength of malice, but the humour and sunshine. Throughout
the thirty-year-long night, jokes have shone, and shine to this
day like stars in the black darkness.

And the underworld ballad could be heard from the farthest
limits of Russia.

These two genres of Russian folklore have both flourished
in the twentieth century – in the most appalling conditions –
and fulfilled in a certain fashion the role of Samizdat (before
anyone dreamed of its existence), by establishing not only the
idea of publication in typescript, but – and this is more
important – the notion of continuity, tradition and development, the process by which one person says something and
writes it down, and a second person picks it up and passes it on.

The future of Russian literature, if it is destined to have a
future at all, has been nourished on political jokes, just as
Pushkin grew up on the fairy tales told by his nanny. In its pure
form, the joke demonstrates the miracle of art, deriving as it
does nothing but good from the savagery and fury of dictators.

* The previous few paragraphs, parts of which are untranslatable,
have been adapted with the help of the author.

So far we have not emerged from the 'semi-folklore' stage, in which literature lacks the strength to spread its wings in book publication and subsists instead on oral forms. But this fate (which is the lot of all suppressed art) is remarkable in its own way, and therefore, as compensation for the lack of the printing press, magazines and the cinema ('And just think of all the things we haven't got! We haven't any oats, we haven't any butter . . .' – from a political joke), we have acquired our singing lyric poets, our troubadours and minstrels – in the form of a brilliant pléiade of poet-singers. I shall not list them by name – the names are in any case universally known, the whole country listens to their songs and sings them, celebrating to guitar accompaniment the birthday of a new, unpublished, unrecorded, accursed, doomed and therefore liberated literature.

> Here I sit with my guitar –
> Open wide the curtain –
> Freedom I shall never see,
> That is our misfortune.
> If you want to, cut my throat,
> Cut my veins and kill me;
> All I beg is – do not cut my
> Seven strings of silver.

That is the sort of thing our truly *popular* poets are singing today. They perform in defiance of the theory and practice of officially imposed 'populism' in art, which coincides, of course, with the concept of '*partiinost*' (party-orientation), which inspires no one, makes a mark on no one's memory and exists in rarefied space – beyond the people and without the people, giving pleasure to no one but the bosses, and then only as long as they are in their offices composing reports to each other and sending them through the proper channels; as soon as those bosses come home, after the usual stiff drinks to buck themselves up after a hard day, they too relax by listening to tape-recorded songs sung to the same solitary guitar that they have just ordered to be smashed. The song has circumvented the impregnable Berlin-type wall which has been erected between literature and the people, and over the past few years it has literally won over the entire country. Here the traditions of the cabaret song and the underworld ballad have somehow merged and given birth to an absolutely special artistic genre, hitherto unknown in Russia, which has replaced the anonymous compositions of folklore by the individual voice of the author, a poet who has dared to sing in the name of the real, not the made-up Russia. If that voice were to be broadcast by radio to the whole country, to the world, the people would have something to rejoice about.

But what *is* being sung on the radio nowadays? Nothing. You may easily confirm this if you wake up early and listen to what is happening in the ether at exactly six a.m. Moscow Time. It is the start of the day, and it naturally begins with the national anthem. Let me try and remember the words:

> Oh Union of free-born republics inviolate,
> United for ever by Russia the Great . . .!

And there it breaks off. No one sings the words any more, or they omit words – because, it turns out, the lines composed by S. Mikhalkov contain too much in praise of Stalin; it would, of course, be a good thing to restore Stalin to his pedestal but the time is not yet ripe, and therefore, since the national anthem cannot be replaced by some other song, people must refrain from using those nice words in praise of the beloved leader. For nearly twenty years Russia has, in effect, existed without her national anthem, and that is why what you hear every morning on the radio is simply a bellowing noise transposed into the braying of wind instruments and brass cymbals. Admittedly it does conjure up a vague impression of something powerful, military and optimistic, but its precise sense cannot be defined. If you happen to be in a prison camp, you have the chance of hearing that tune every day, broadcast simultaneously by all the camp loudspeakers and amplifiers instead of reveille. For the sake of objectivity I should add that on each occasion these clarion sounds are mingled with the more melodious, though somewhat depressing noise of someone striking a length of rail (see *One Day in the Life of Ivan Denisovich*) and in an amazing way these two bell-tones – internal and external – interact with each other, so that when heard at home the national anthem gives a man the definite feeling that nothing has changed and that he has woken up again in a hut behind barbed wire. Morning in Mother Russia.

Every historical fact is symbolic and twenty years of brassy booming instead of words, which many people are still itching to sing, are also symbolic, and therefore, when reflecting on the present status of the national anthem, you come to the inevitable conclusion that for a long time now Russia has been frozen in some kind of interim phase, in which nothing new has emerged, while the old order has retreated and lacks the strength to say anything clear and forceful to frighten its enemies.

Yet there was a time (also at dawn; the dawn of the Soviet régime) when words were used more or less successfully, despite the fact that the Party leaders of the time were desperately overworked and, what is more, had no ear or feeling whatsoever for the development of the language. This latter factor made itself felt in the multitude of words which were coined in the early Soviet era, and which sounded like some crude abracadabra, more apt to frighten people than to encourage them to take part in building the great new system. All those acronyms like: 'VTsik', 'TsiK', 'Rabkrin', 'Gubispolkom' and 'Narobraz',* independently of the will of their creators, really did exude some kind of lethal miasma, especially at night. Yet despite the leadership's deafness to music and poetry, at least three good words did make their appearance, which can only be explained by the intervention of divine grace (and therefore, unlike purely destructive critics, I believe that in the beginning, the revolution, while not exactly full of sweetness and light, was absolutely inevitable). While enjoining its citizens to hold their tongues, the young state nevertheless managed to implant in the national consciousness three good words, which are worth analysing in detail because they possess a higher meaning.

The first word is 'Bolshevik' (not to be confused with 'communist'). 'Bolshevik' implies 'more' or 'bigger', and 'bigger' is always good. The bigger the better. I am profoundly convinced that the failure of the Mensheviks was entirely due to the fact that they inscribed on their banners a word implying 'less' or 'smaller'. Therefore the Russian people chose the one that was 'bigger'.

The second word is *Cheká*. The Extraordinary Commission [the original euphemism for the secret police]. Neither 'commission' nor 'extraordinary' speak to the Russian heart; but *cheká*

* These are acronyms for various early Soviet institutions.

is a word that promises much good, because it implies being 'on the alert' (*nachekú*). And one must always be on the alert. The fact that the present-day State Security forces are trying to resurrect that word – *cheká* and *chekist* – does not only indicate that they want to recall the romance of the revolution and the clean hands of Dzerzhinsky (although in fact his hands probably *were* cleaner than those of any of his successors); the word *cheká* in itself is expressive. It has a firmness, a certain crispness. It is a word you can rely on; it won't let you down. It was in prison camp that I first heard the word *chekist* pronounced with a peculiar disgust (as in the underworld ballad: 'From the watch tower looks down/The hated *chekist* . . .'). But outside prison – I frankly admit it – the word enjoys a great popularity.

The third word, or rather expression, is the most important and the most cherished: 'Soviet power'. That good ship has sailed far and is still seaworthy. The fact that there is no Soviet power is immaterial. Everyone has known for a long time that it does not exist, and they have managed very well without it. The important thing is not who is actually running the government and waving to the crowds from the top of Lenin's tomb: the important thing is the word *Soviet* – a good word and packed with meaning. [Some of the most significant associations and undertones of 'Soviet' in Russian are:]

1. *Soviet* → *svet* ['light' or 'world']
   svet → *svetly* ['bright, radiant, pure']
2. *Soviet* → *svoi* ['our own']
   svoie → *svoyak* ['brother-in-law' or 'close friend']

In other words, '*Soviet*' = *ours*, which means *good*. To this day cases occur where a peasant will heap violent abuse on the 'communists' but at the same time will stoutly defend 'Soviet power'. And that is not some sophisticated political argument as to which is preferable – 'the Soviets' or 'the Party'; it is simply an opposition based on the *sound* of words: '*Who* needs your *Communists*,* when we have our (*svoya*) Soviet (*sovetskaya*) power standing behind us? All of us here are on *our side* (*svoi*) – and outsiders have no business here.'

* In Russian the dative case of the relative pronoun 'who' is 'komu', which sounds like the first two syllables of the word 'kommunist'.

It is on these three words, as on the backs of three whales, that the régime has rested and rests to this day. Therefore what I have to say here is in no way an attempt to undermine the régime (as many people may think), but is instead a piece of advice: pay more attention to the literary language. For what has happened in recent years? There has been no poetry, not a trace of inventiveness. A whole town, for instance, was named after Palmiro Togliatti;* yet the people who went to live in that Palmyra called it, in their simple, Soviet fashion, *Telyatin.†* Or take all those fashionable strings of initials, which are enough to try the patience and ingenuity of an archangel and can easily drive mere mortals insane, reducing them to profane and irresponsible language. For example, once we had VKPB‡, now we have KGB. At first sight there is nothing much wrong in the change; the new version even has a more lapidary ring to it. But the outcome of such innovations is always to blur the picture of who is really running the country. Where will it all lead? Where do Lenin and Stalin stand now? And what is S. Mikhalkov to do, who must express all these reforms in verse? And then you must admit, comrades, that on sober reflection the letters KGB don't sound very poetic to the Russian ear, either. KGB is slightly reminiscent of crematoria and coffins, or at best it conjures up the footsteps of the Commendatore treading over gravestones. And just think what the end result of all these verbal experiments could be!

Would it not have been better to have let Russia keep the earlier word forms – with the 'Bolshevik' in charge, directing 'Soviet power' from above with the help of the *Cheká*? In my opinion it would have sounded better, and most important of all – it would have been a great deal simpler and more accessible to ordinary people.

I apologise for these layman's excursions into politics and linguistics, but you must agree that without the words under discussion the literary process in Russia would be – to put it mildly – incomprehensible. Because when you read books

---

* Togliatti (1893–1964) was leader of the Italian Communist Party for nearly forty years.

† A phonetic approximation to 'Togliatti' derived from the Russian word 'telyatina', which means 'veal'.

‡ These initials represent 'The All-Russian Communist Party (Bolsheviks)'.

distributed by Samizdat, very often, and particularly at first sight, you get the impression that because of overwork the members of the leadership have simply not found time to read these books, otherwise they would undoubtedly have stopped short, come to their senses and made some changes in their catastrophic régime. For these books – in their style, in the facts they reveal and in their appeal to mankind's better feelings – are so much more persuasive and convincing than those innumerable official directives which descend from on high in a ceaseless, silent flow, their contents devoid of the slightest attempt to discover what is actually happening in the real world.

It is at this point that literature must be on its guard and must not give way to the seductive spell of speaking the truth and nothing but the truth. The danger threatening modern Russian literature – banned literature, of course (the other literature is not worth considering, since artistically it is about two hundred years out of date) – is of assuming the role of a sort of whining complaints book, supposedly to be perused by the leaders (who don't give a damn anyway), or to be stored away in a cupboard until the advent of those better times when people will have learned to live by the light of truth. This attitude is one of the chronic failings of the nineteenth century, which we have inherited from two books with interrogative titles: *Who is to Blame?* and *What is to be Done?** We are again faced by the eternal Russian dilemma: where is your allegiance, you professional purveyors of culture? Whose side are you on? Are you for truth, or for the official lie? When the question is put like that, the writer obviously has no choice but to answer proudly: for truth! And that is the only fitting reply in such a situation. But in proclaiming oneself to be on the side of truth, it is worthwhile remembering what Stalin said when some brave members of the Union of Writers asked him to explain once and for all what socialist realism was, and how, in practical terms, to attain those glittering heights. Without taking a moment's thought or batting an eyelid, the leader replied:

'Write the truth – and that will be socialist realism!'

---

* Two classic nineteenth-century Russian novels of social analysis and protest written respectively by Alexander Herzen (1812–1870) and Nikolai Chernyshevsky (1828–1889).

The point has been reached where we should fear the truth, lest it hang round our necks again like an albatross. Let the writer refuse to tell lies, but let him create fiction – and in disregard of any kind of 'realism'. Otherwise all this promising, liberated literature will again be reduced to a recital of the torments we suffer and the remedies we offer in their place. It will revert to those questions: 'What is to be done?' and 'Who is to blame?' And everything will fall to pieces and it will begin all over again: 'liberation movement' – 'naturalist school' – 'realist school' – and as the natural culmination we shall end up again with 'Party literature', with writers, in Lenin's words, acting as 'screws and cogwheels' in the 'common proletarian cause'. It would be a good thing to avoid all that; to refrain from offering ready-made recipes. Having exorcised ourselves from the lie, we have no right to succumb to the temptation of the truth, which will lead us back to socialist realism inside out. We must put a stop to our cringing and currying favour with that hectoring taskmaster – reality! After all, we *are* writers, artists in words.

Isn't it time to renounce the magic of words like 'realism' and 'communism'? Isn't it time we took these things out of quotation marks as a matter of course? A young man once appeared in my house and said: 'I am an anti-communist! I am for the truth!' At the time, it sounded splendid: here was someone who wasn't afraid to speak out. Later, however, doubts and analogies came to mind. Suppose someone were to go around repeating: 'I am an anti-fascist!' Very nice . . . except that it is somehow too commonplace, unconvincing, cheap. Why take as the yardstick of your own value something which you find worthless? How can you define yourself in relation to a negative? We shall never break away from 'realism-communism' if we are constantly glancing back at those words. We don't say: 'I'm an anti-liar!' or 'I'm anti-beast, anti-mass-murderer!' If you are a man, why do you need to go on proving every day that you have long since evolved beyond the animal state?

Because I am, I must confess, rather suspicious of realism; I have a feeling that a new lie might develop from it. Our age has taught us that there are times when we should beware the righteous man more than the known informer. When an informer looks at you, he is wondering whether to shop you now or whether it might be to his advantage to wait a bit. The righteous enthusiast, however, will risk his life to rush in and point the finger at you. Ah, those lovely girls who braved all to mount the rostrum at Komsomol meetings:

'Andrei, stand up and answer in front of everybody – tell the *truth* with absolute frankness: what did you say to me about collective farms before you kissed me yesterday? Come on, own up – as a matter of principle!'

Ah, those honest, upright, blue-eyed girls. . . . There is *realism* for you!

So perhaps we'll try and take it out of quotation marks (and throw it on the scrap-heap), shall we?

I realise that everything I have just said will evaporate like hot air or lyric poetry; I realise that oppression by the state is still too severe for us to break away and emancipate ourselves from 'communism' and 'realism'. Our self-perception is still too conditional, too negative, and our excuse for it is – oppression.

Not long ago in Russia some writers were decorated with the Alexander Fadeyev* Medal for Courage. Fadeyev, as everyone knows from the newspapers and from official comments on his premature death, committed suicide as a result of chronic alcoholism and did nothing worthy of his gold medal – except perhaps for having, towards the end, repented of the harm he had done to Russian literature. Involuntarily, a question comes to mind. How long can a large and independent state do without art and literature? For no sooner do art and literature begin to emerge through the feeble medium of Samizdat, than the state regards it as its first and chief duty to destroy them, by letting loose generals, steelworkers, welders and the like, who can easily dispose of writers and their paper paraphernalia. It is perhaps understandable that Czechoslovakia, a small and not wholly independent country, has managed to exist these last few years, it is said, without any literature at all; the Czechs don't seem to mind, their country flourishes and feels no shame. But we are not Czechoslovakia. We could, if you'll pardon the expression, eat Czechoslovakia before breakfast. And compared with us, what are Madagascar or New Guinea, countries which will also fall into our clutches before too long? 'What need have we

* Fadeyev is well known for his strict obedience to the Soviet authorities.

of Africa!' – as the officially approved song has it. We shall seize Africa, seize America – splendid! And what will we have to show for it? The Alexander Fadeyev Medal for Courage?

All this is like the electrocardiogram of a weakening heart. It is like a monologue in front of a completely silent television screen. The sound is switched off and no words are heard coming from the screen, but you can see someone reading from a paper and waving his arms, while other people march and applaud each other in reply to soundless speeches. After looking at it for a long time, the suspicion begins to creep in that perhaps, just as we in front of the screen can hear nothing, *they* can neither hear nor understand anything of what is going on here, among those of us involved in the literary process – we who are constantly trying to explain something to our government and offering for its attention book after book, which seem to us remarkable, absolutely irrefutable and constructive, but which simply never come within earshot of those shadowy figures on the screen. Books to them are inaudible, unnecessary. By this, I am trying to describe the interrelation between literature and society in Russia.

In our prison camp there was a group of youths from the remote provinces who had been convicted for composing leaflets that were communist in sympathy but which, of course, advocated certain proposals for moderating and popularising the régime. Having distributed their revolutionary leaflets, before they were arrested our young Komsomols passed a resolution: to buy a new pair of trousers and shoes for their leader, whose clothes and shoes were somewhat worn out. They then spent all their spare time in front of a television set, carefully watching all the programmes broadcast from Moscow – in order not to miss the historic moment when the government, once having read their leaflets and grasped their meaning, would appeal by radio and television for moral support to their young well-wishers, who were naturally living a semi-underground existence and thus temporarily inaccessible to the eye of authority. They were waiting, that is to say, until the government, touched to the heart by such truthful, just and socially useful leaflets, should send out a call and invite them to Moscow. Hence the need for new trousers and shoes – to wear at the meeting with members of the government.

All this is simply a set of variations on my original theme: the belief in the power of words. Everyone shares this belief: the common people, the writers, the authorities (who, having investigated the leaflets, immediately, as the rules prescribe, arrested and imprisoned the young truth-seekers), as well as the writers of those countless letters, complaints and appeals to those same authorities. That is why people write, and why they are forbidden to write. That is why others are silent and why the authorities put people in prison. Apart from the sad and comic aspects of this business, it also reveals the existence of certain very positive characteristics, inherent in Russian life and Russian literature. To us, words are still too alive, too passionate, too solid and active in their internal secretions to treat them coolly, as people do in the West – where words are spoken and written, it seems, without any particular hindrance, but also without any great passion on the part of the speaker or writer. For our problems are completely incomprehensible to those in the West. They cannot understand why it is necessary to destroy someone for writing words, nor why the larger, official body of writers, that vast literary army, cannot utter a word without looking round to make sure that it agrees with the intentions and permitted phraseology of higher authority. Nor why from time to time something goes wrong in the ranks of that army, and someone dashes out and starts shouting, as furiously as though he thought he were about to turn the world upside down.

The West's attitude to us is the same as our attitude to the Chinese. Do we shed many tears over China? Only in so far as it will make the Chinese leave us alone; as long as they do that, they can do what else they like. They can denounce Confucius to their hearts' content, if that amuses them, while we are prepared to unload on them everything from our own lumber room that is most ugly and absurd – much good may it do them. Beggars can't be choosers. China was always a strange sort of place; presumably it suits the Chinese – anyway, they're used to it.

However, while taking a sceptical attitude to any hopes of changing or improving anything in this world by the power of words, we must nevertheless make use of our age-old, purely Russian habit of treating words as real (as though words themselves were the actual deeds for which people are put up against a wall and shot), so that on this fertile, well-manured soil we may try and cultivate something astonishing, something exotic – if not in the physical, then in the literary sense. We may not be able to move the mountain, but a fairy tale, perhaps, may arise instead.

When Arkady Belinkov was arrested (it was, I think, in 1944) for writing a novel which never did get published, his interrogator sent the manuscript to be reviewed by two of the country's foremost literary scholars – to E. Kovalchik (she headed the Department of Soviet Literature at Moscow University) and to B. Yermilov. The reviews were written at a high academic level – the whole novel was subjected to a complete dissection, including even analyses of the style – and ended, in practical terms; in a single verdict:

'Mad dogs should be shown no mercy!'

This workers' slogan was picked up and adopted by academic philologists as long ago as the mid-thirties, when the firing-squads were hard at work. Thus wherever we may look, we see Russia's astounding capacity to take the writer at face value, to read grave threats to the system into his fictional images. And it is this capacity, I say, which ought to be utilised.

There is no need to quote only negative examples. In the history of literature there is no shortage of evidence for the way in which writers have nobly fulfilled their duty to their country. At the memorial gathering held one evening in honour of the poet Eduard Bagritsky* (it was after the death of Stalin, but before the total denunciation of the cult of his personality), a writer called Mark Kolosov – now dead but in his time a very combative journalist in the Komsomol press – described the following episode to a group of young people, who listened in amazement. He had once lived on the same landing as Bagritsky and they had been good friends. One evening Bagritsky's telephone rang and the voice of an unknown agent of State Security proposed that Bagritsky should report to a certain address at midnight, keeping this summons a secret even from the members of his own family. So despite their long-standing friendship Bagritsky revealed nothing of this to his neighbour

* Bagritsky (1895–1934) was a Soviet poet and translator of poetry.

and meticulously observed the instructions passed to him by telephone. That neighbour, however, being a trusted Party member, already knew what was afoot and made a point of dropping in on his friend Eduard that evening – just to see what lies he might make up at the approach of midnight. At about eleven o'clock Bagritsky started to get nervous, to glance at his watch, and seeing that his visitor was not going to leave, finally announced morosely that he proposed to take a walk. Smiling, Kolosov offered to keep him company, particularly since he, too, had been given similar instructions the previous day and simply wanted to test his famous friend's ability to keep a secret. What a scene then ensued! Bagritsky shouted at Kolosov to leave him in peace: he wanted to be alone. . . . An hour later they met face to face in Gorky's house, whither many of the most distinguished Soviet writers had been summoned by a similar phone call – for a friendly meeting with Stalin. That night a new statute, a new passport was issued to Soviet literature: 'socialist realism'.

While Mark Kolosov went on to fill in his portrait of Eduard Bagritsky (his honesty, his integrity, his ability to keep military secrets and so on), we, his listeners, were able to picture to ourselves that truly remarkable scene, which enabled us to grasp certain of the essential, though almost imperceptible links from which, like a chain, the literary process was made up. Imagine for yourself, reader, a night in Moscow of the early thirties, through which the writers – 'engineers of human souls',* – crept like thieves from every part of the capital, hiding from each other, having been summoned by a police telephone call and kept in total ignorance of why they were wanted in such secrecy. Now *that* is an instance of what was called consolidation; *that* is how, merely by appealing to the sinister, nocturnal streak in his mentality, the writer is made security conscious, made conscious that Russian literature is not a normal pastime like eating soup, nor is it just scribbling with pen on paper, but is something immeasurably more responsible and infinitely forbidden.

Admittedly it is impossible nowadays to resurrect the inner strength and faith which motivated those writers who gathered one by one, at night, with such delicious fear, under Gorky's

* Stalin's phrase.

roof. Today, rather, writers creep away by night in many different directions. A process of break-up and dispersal has begun in Soviet literature. But even in that break-up one can detect the purposive operation (but in different directions) of the process which in the past was known as consolidation. Security consciousness, on the other hand, has grown to even greater dimensions. And again – why not make use of these splendid qualities, which are obviously organically inherent in the Russian spirit, for the good of the cause, having confined that cause (at least for the time being) to the level of – words? What novels, plays and poems would pour forth! How we would once more astonish the world by the enigma of the Russian soul!

Russian books (if one considers them at a serious level) have always been written in blood, and in that lies their superiority, their primacy in world literature. That is why the officially-published literature – 'Gosizdat'* – is losing in the competition with 'Samizdat', although the forces involved are far from equal. And that, too, is why Stalin, who had an excellent grasp of human psychology, arranged for writers such suitably artistic stage settings as those conspiratorial gatherings in a 'safe house', after which writers, like heroes, were naturally ready to offer themselves in selfless sacrifice.

Nowadays we have come to our senses and choose our own form of sacrifice. What vast resources of talent, though, Russia must possess, for the history of her literature – which is on the whole a comparatively peaceful, sedentary occupation – to have been filled with corpses; for the whole course of the country's development, almost since Ivan the Terrible (though we can't remember so far back – memory fails us) to have proceeded not by way of the accumulation and preservation of values, but by way of schism – when whole families, classes, categories of the population (for instance, the 'Raskolniki'†), often precisely the most talented, morally sensitive and worth-while people, likely to bring renown to the nation – were either periodically destroyed or flung out like so much rubbish. And yet how rich the country must be in order so generously,

* This acronym means 'state publishing', as opposed to 'self-publishing'.

† A group of religious schismatics of the seventeenth century.

so wastefully to scatter its human reserves and then, depleted, to replenish itself again – for a new harvest, a new diaspora.

Today the 'Third Emigration' is in the news, the third to take place under Soviet rule, the third in fifty-seven years. So far, the overwhelming majority of these emigrés are Jews, who are being allowed out relatively easily. But if everyone were allowed to leave, no one knows which nationality would predominate: Lithuanians, Latvians, Russians or Ukrainians. It is a good thing that the Jews, at least, are being let go; not simply because it is the migration of a people to their historic homeland, but above all because it is a flight from Russia. It means that Russia has grown unbearable for them; it means they can't take it any more. Some of them go out of their minds when they break out into freedom; some of them lapse into poverty as they look for a suitable niche for a Russian in the vast, unfamiliar, stifling outside world. But still they leave. One day Mother Russia, you bitch, you will have to answer for these children of yours, whom you brought up and then shamefully flung onto the rubbish-heap.

Russia, of course, will manage without Jews, just as she has managed without a church, without a nobility, without an intelligentsia, without literature. She has, in the end, the strength and the means to make good this latest loss too. It is still an empire, with countless different peoples: Tartars, Chuvash, Greeks, and even Assyrians. What will it be like without Jews? It will be boring, monochrome. And who then will be the scapegoat for our familiar sins?

This is perhaps the right place for me to say a few words in defence of Russian anti-Semitism. By that I mean – what good is concealed, in the psychological sense, in the unfriendly Russian attitude (putting it at its mildest) towards the Jews? The Russian is incapable of admitting that any evil can derive from a Russian, because deep down (like everyone, no doubt) within his soul he is good. He cannot conceive that in the Russian state Russian people can be made unhappy through the fault of other Russians or by his own fault. A Russian is one of us, ours (*svoi, svoisky, sovietsky*; see above). Nothing bad ever comes from *our* people, always from others. Russian anti-Semitism is a way of externalising evil, a way of thrusting our own sins onto a scapegoat.

Obviously this is not much comfort to the Jews. But in this instance I would ask you also to consider the moral problem of the Russian, who, having done so much harm to himself and to others, simply cannot work out how it all happened – unless it is due to interference by some kind of 'wreckers', 'spies' and 'saboteurs', who have secretly seized power and have turned everything that was good in the Russians into bad. In prison camps, for instance, simple peasants (especially among the long-term prisoners) are convinced to this day that the entire government of present-day Russia, all the judges, all the state prosecutors – and above all the KGB – consist entirely of Jews. To explain to them that nowadays a Jew simply cannot reach such heights, that the Jews themselves are having a hard time, is impossible. The decisive argument is as follows:

'Don't tell me you believe a *Russian* could give a twenty-five-year sentence for *nothing*, do you? Only a *Jew* could do that.'

It is pointless to stress the purely Russian names of the country's rulers. '*We* know them – they have all changed their names to disguise themselves. Ah, those Yids – I hate 'em!' It is equally pointless to show the portraits, printed in *Pravda*, of members of the Politbureau, the Central Committee or the Presidium of the Supreme Soviet, where the dominant features are the fat, snub-nosed, ingenuous mugs of typical Great Russians.

'Huh – hook-nosed Yid. Just look at him – a typical Yid.'

Lest I be accused of defamation, I shall not mention the names of those respected, hundred per cent Russian comrades to whom those comments referred.

References to the Soviet Union's policy, known to everyone from the newspapers, of supporting the Arabs in the Arab-Israeli war, do no good either. '*We* know – they're secretly helping Israel all the same! You don't know what snakes they are!' And yet at the same time – during the Six Day War, for instance – all their sympathy was for Israel: it's nice when a little 'un gives a beating to a big 'un . . .

This is not primitive ignorance or lack of culture, as many Jews think. It is an effort to shield oneself against an all-penetrating, ubiquitous spectre: it is the urge to renounce evil. There is no point in being naïve and hoping (as some Jews hope) that anti-Semitism in Russia is something entirely imposed from above by the powers of the state, a seed planted in the soil of blindness and ignorance. Ah, but your Russian peasant is not quite so ignorant and he is definitely not blind. He has known for a long time that Lenin was a Jew, as was Stalin (a Georgian Jew), and even Leo Tolstoy (yes, I have actually heard this said). Some perplexity is admittedly caused by the examples of Ivan the Terrible and his *oprichnina*,* Genghiz Khan and Mao Tse-tung, who, despite all the trouble they have caused, cannot with the best will in the world be classified as Jews (still – you never know). In other words, in the popular consciousness the Jew is an evil spirit. He is the devil, who has covertly invaded the virtuous body of Russia and has made everything go wrong. The Jew is an objectivisation of Russia's original sin, from which she for ever longs to purge herself but cannot.

It must not be thought that this derives only from memories of the revolution, the twenties or thirties, when Jews played a far from minor part in Russian history. The theme is a larger one, of much wider import, even, than the Soviet régime. It is, if you like, a metaphysical quality of the Russian soul, which tries time and again (and the revolution occurred because of this) to return to a primordial state of paradise. And it never works: there is always some 'Yid' to disturb and muddle all the cards. The 'Yid' is at large somewhere amongst us, behind us and, as sometimes happens, within ourselves. The 'Yid' squeezes and worms his way in everywhere and ruins everything. 'Don't act the Yid!' is a heartfelt saying, made with the implied assumption that a Russian ought not to be, cannot be bad. 'We're infested with Yids!' people will say, as though talking about lice or cockroaches. If only we could get rid of them!

They are indeed hard to get rid of. A Tartar, for example, or a gypsy – you can recognise them a mile off and you can treat them in your own, Russian, more or less simple, comprehensible (i.e. Soviet) way. But a Yid looks almost like a Russian . . . Almost? You can't always spot him at first sight – you may even take him for Ivan Ivanovich. The Yid is crafty and evasive (what else can he be?); you have to be able to sniff him out and recognise him for what he is. The Yid is the hidden irritant

---

* The *oprichniki* were Ivan's praetorian guard, an early version of the Russian secret police.

in the peaceful life of Russia, which, were there no Yids, would all go smoothly. And if those demons would only go away, we should be in paradise . . .

The present anti-Semitic policy of the régime is based to a great extent on that popular conception (and for that reason the policy cannot be called 'anti-popular'), namely that you only have to reject evil and anathematise it in the guise of 'bourgeoisie', 'right-wing' or 'left-wing' deviation, or by calling them 'fascists', 'enemies of the people', 'murderers in white coats', or more simply 'Yids', and then the era of peace and bliss will come, because within ourselves, among 'our own kind' we are all good, civilised people – and only the 'Yids' are preventing this from coming to pass.

If in a prison camp the political officer says to a young man, imprisoned as a 'specially dangerous state criminal' for 'anti-Soviet agitation and propaganda' (and says it sincerely, with pain in his voice):

'How dare you not go to political lectures when such an intense ideological struggle is going on all over the world at this moment?'

If an outsider lecturer, visiting a prison camp, turns to his audience, consisting entirely of spies, saboteurs, terrorists and fervent anti-Soviet agitators, and says in a near-whisper:

'Our relations with China are now extremely complex and tense. Only I must ask you to keep this between ourselves . . .'

. . . then these remarks imply that we are all on 'our' side, all 'soviet' people (what else could they be?) and quarrels must be kept in the family. 'Imperialists', who live in unattainable, outer space (all this is excellently mapped out and explained by Kozma Indikoplov in his *Topography*) are simply hankering after our country and our souls: those 'imperialists' are the Yids, the whole of the outside world is made up of Yids, but we shall never give in to them at any price!

Once, it seems, Saltykov-Shchedrin* made a joke at the expense of the 'enemy within'. Nowadays in Russia it is the Yid who is the chief 'enemy within', who is best expelled beyond the perimeter (the casting out of demons) and then (it is much more easily done 'outside') – crushed by tanks. And to this end,

---

* Saltykov-Shchedrin (1826–1889) was a well-known Russian satirical writer.

presumably, we are meanwhile sending our tanks to the Arabs for good measure.

You ask me what all this has to do with Russian literature. Particularly since I declare that, apart from artistic concerns, I have no claims to make whatever. A legitimate question; and I, barking like a dog and down on all fours, will try to answer it.

Firstly, the Jewish question has the most immediate, direct connection with the literary process – because every Russian writer (of Russian origin) who at the present time refuses to write to order is a Jew. He is a black sheep, an enemy of the people. I believe that if they now (at last) start killing Jews in Russia, the first people to be murdered will be writers and intellectuals of non-Jewish origin, who for one reason or another do not come into the category of 'our man'. In a broader sense, too, every writer – be he a Frenchman, Englishman or American, who are under no threat – is a Jew who should be beaten up (and then, perhaps, he might write something).

Secondly, the current Jewish exodus from Russia coincides to a great extent with the steady outflow of manuscripts from Russia. Just think of those manuscripts crossing the frontier. Each one is running a risk. Each one of them is already entered in the list of things to be destroyed, like those Jews who disturb and ruin our lives. Imagine how those manuscripts feel as they escape from Russia and have no idea what to do with themselves outside. Everything has been left behind in Russia: all the pain, which enabled us to write . . . Jews! Brothers! – how many of us are there left? A mere handful.

When we left Russia – we left quietly, among a party of Jews – I noticed my books bouncing about on the plank floor of the lorry taking us to the customs house. The books had been tied up in bundles, and as they bounced I caught glimpses of their titles: *Poets of the Renaissance*, *The Art of Ancient Pskov*. At that moment I had mentally rejected them all. But they still went on bouncing. The complete works of Saltykov-Shchedrin, whom I do not like and never have liked, given to me by a friend of my youth, from whom I had parted company after a confrontation in court. My books, too, were emigrating, whether they wanted to or not. The houses and streets of Moscow, where my books and I had spent all our lives, rolled past. We sped past the new monument to Lermontov, in the pose of a smart young officer. But the books in their bundles continued to bounce around me and repeated: 'Farewell.' I was taking these books away on my own responsibility, not knowing what awaited them, promising them nothing. I was only glad, as I looked at the package of little brown volumes, that Mikhail Yevgrafovich Saltykov-Shchedrin, muffled up to the ears, was leaving with us.

The lorry bounced violently; the floor beneath us and the books swayed and bumped. We were leaving for ever. Everything was over, everything forgotton. And only one of us, whom I had never liked, Mikhail Yevgrafovich, was hanging back, although he was bouncing too.

We drove out to Kalanchyovka. The far distance opened out to our future adventures. The books bounced. And getting out too, hunching his ears into his coat collar, was Mikhail Yevgrafovich Saltykov-Shchedrin himself, in person . . .

Paris, June 1974

Three Poems

JOSEPH BRODSKY

The End of a Beautiful Era

Because the art of poetry makes words necessary,
I, one of the deaf, balding, dismal emissaries
    of a second-rate power, caught up in this
and not wishing to do violence to my brain,
am outfitting myself and heading down to the kiosk
    to see what the evening papers contain.

Wind whips the leaves. The dimness of old lamp bulbs in these
sad parts, whose motto is 'the mirror's triumph' breeds
    an illusion of abundance with the help of puddles.
Even thieves steal oranges by first scraping the amalgam off
the mirror's back. Yet the feeling you have when you huddle
    before your image, this feeling I have lost.

Everything in these sad parts is geared for winter: prison walls,
dreams, overcoats, bridal dresses – the snowfall's
    whiteness at New Year's, the second-hands of clocks,
lean, grey jackets, equal measures of mud for soap, linen,
puritanical mores, and wooden hand-warmers tucked
    in the hands of violinists.

This land is motionless. Imagining the output of lead
and cast-iron, and shaking your stupefied head,
    you recall the former power of bayonet and Cossack whip.
But the eagles come to rest like lodestone on the scraps;
even wicker chairs here are made to fit
    by means of nuts and bolts.

Only the fish in the sea know freedom's price,
but their muteness compels us as if we must devise
    cashier booths and labels of our own. And space climbs
as dearly as a bill of fare. Time is created by death; its search
for bodily properties leads to raw vegetables first,
    a cock takes its cue from the chimes.

Unfortunately to live in our era and stay elevated, alert,
and sensitive is hard. When you have just raised a skirt
    you see no sweet marvels, but what you sought instead,
nor will Lobachevsky's* parallels help to make this clear,
but widened horizons too must somehow be unspread,
    and the end of perspective is here.

Either Europe's map has been swiped by plainclothes agents
or the remaining five-sixths is, from here, too distant;
    or in fact a certain good fairy is present
and conjures over me, – but I can't escape this city.
I pour myself Cahors – forgoing the servant –
    and rub my ordinary kitty.

Either my temple should get a bullet – precisely in the place
of error – by pointing a finger, or I should steal away
    on the water like a new Christ. How can you be blamed
for confusing a train with a ship when you're drunk, eyes glazed,
and you're frost-battered? Still, you won't burn from shame.
    Like a boat on water, the train wheel leaves no trace.

What are the papers declaring from the Hall of Justice?
The sentence is carried out to the letter. Just as
    a local resident peers through his bulky glasses he sees
a man lying face-down beside a wall,
but not asleep: his dreams have a right to be
    disgusted at the perforations in his skull.

* The creator of non-Euclidic geometry (1792–1856).

The keensightedness of our era is entwined by roots turning
to times incapable in their common blindness of discerning
　　those fallen from cradles from dropped pipes.
The ancestor Chud doesn't want to look beyond his own demise.
So many plates, a pity, and no one to revolve the table
　　to make you rise, Rurik, and be answerable.

The keensightedness of these times is vigilance to a dead end.
For now, it's not fitting for thought to range over a tree when
　　spit is on the wall, and not to wake a prince: but a dinosaur.
For the last line: don't pluck a bird's feathers.
The only thing for an unrepentant head is to wait for
　　the axe and green laurel together.

Leningrad, 1969

In the Lake District

In those days, in a place where dentists thrive
(their daughters order fancy clothes from London;
their painted forceps hold aloft on signboards
a common and abstracted wisdom tooth),
there I – whose mouth held ruins more abject
than any Parthenon – a spy, a spearhead
for some fifth column of a rotting culture
(my cover was a lit-professorship),
was living at a college near the most
renowned of the fresh-water lakes; my function,
which I performed on Tuesdays, was to wear out
the patience of the ingenuous local youth.
Whatever I wrote then was incomplete;
my lines expired in strings of dots. Collapsing,
I dropped, still fully dressed, upon my bed.
At night I stared up at the darkened ceiling
until I saw a shooting star, which then,
conforming to the laws of self-combustion,
would flash – before I'd even made a wish –
across my cheek and down onto my pillow.

Ann Arbor, 1972–3

On the Death of Zhukov*

Columns of grandsons, stiff at attention;
gun-carriage, coffin, riderless horse.
Wind brings no sound of their glorious Russian
trumpets, their weeping trumpets of war.
Splendid regalia deck out the corpse:
thundering Zhukov rolls toward death's mansion.

As a commander, making walls crumble,
he held a sword less sharp than his foe's.
Brilliant manœuvres across Volga flatlands
set him with Hannibal. And his last days
found him, like Pompey, fallen and humbled –
like Belisarius banned and disgraced.

How much dark blood, soldier's blood, did he spill then
on alien fields? Did he weep for his men?
As he lay dying, did he recall them –
swathed in civilian white sheets at the end?
He gives no answer. What will he tell them,
meeting in Hell? 'We were fighting to win.'

Zhukov's right arm, which once was enlisted
in a just cause, will battle no more.
Sleep! Russian history holds, as is fitting,
space for the exploits of those who, though bold,
marching triumphant through foreign cities,
shook with cold terror when they came home.

Marshal! These words will be swallowed by Lethe,
utterly lost, like your rough soldier's boots.

* This poem was inspired by Derzhavin's celebrated poem *Snegir'*
('The Bullfinch') written, in May 1800, on the death of Count A. V.
Suvorov, commander of the Russian armies under Catherine the Great.
The bullfinch's song is supposed to resemble the sound of a fife. The
metre of both poems suggests the slow interrupted beat of a military
funeral march.

Still, take this tribute, though it is little,
to one who somehow – here I speak truth
plain and aloud – has saved our embattled
homeland. Drum, beat! And shriek out, bullfinch-fife!

London, 1974

The Story of the Marriage of Ivan Petrovich

A Narrative

VLADIMIR MARAMZIN

'Two unfortunates existing in a state of friendship
are like unto two frail saplings that, in leaning on
each other, can more easily withstand storms and
all sorts of fierce winds.' KOZMA PRUTKOV

Part One

A SPIRIT NOT ONE'S OWN

'. . . but don't you destroy her, let her spirit be of mine
and we shall come to terms about the rest.'
    'All right . . . let her spirit be of yours, but her flesh
of mine.'

FOLK TALES OF LAPLAND

1 Ivan Petrovich

I

Ivan Petrovich looked at his photographs of childhood. He liked
himself most at the age of twelve. Here was a boy with close-
cropped hair, who did not strike a stranger's eye or even have
the will to, and whose face absolutely melted with purity. This
purity – like that of a complete stranger – seemed amazing to
Ivan Petrovich. It was not the languid purity of a dreamer or
of someone who loves to live because it's hard to; or of someone
who wants to seem purer than he actually is. It was simply that
the person appearing before him was a natural man at that
age, incapable of living other than in purity; and purity
reciprocated by shining steadily in his face and attracting
others. But the destruction of this purity was very soon accomplished – within ten years or so – and most of the blame for
this he laid on women, whom he had soon been attracted to and
begun thinking about, getting burned by his sincere regard for
them, by his ardour, and receiving in return very precise
knowledge of the rules of the game.

'I'll never ever forgive them for it,' Ivan Petrovich thought,
perturbed, but somehow he always forgot not to forgive.

II

On the whole, Ivan Petrovich was an uncommonly truthful

person, and this often worked against him. At first he had studied to be an electrical engineer. He had made it to the third year, but he just couldn't imagine an electron. The explanation of it kept getting more and more complicated, and there were few who could conceive of it fully. What was it? – both wave and particle.

'You've just got to believe in it, that's all there is to it,' everyone told Ivan Petrovich.

'No,' Ivan Petrovich would answer sadly. 'How can I believe in it if I can't imagine it? And I can't be an engineer if I can't imagine an electron.'

'Accept it as an axiom, for heaven's sake!', people would say to him, laughing at him.

'You've only got to believe in it once and be done with it,' the Assistant Dean tried to convince him.

'Come off it! Stop playing coy. You've got to believe in it!' said the junior members of the faculty, the students, the trade-union organiser, the Young Communist League organiser, the Communist Party organiser, the engineers, the cloakroom girl, his mother, the girl lab assistants, Missy Natasha at the snack bar, the entrance-hall porter, and the conductor on the trolleybus.

'No, I can't,' he would reply apologetically. 'I've really got to imagine it. It's the electron, after all. Everything is based on it, all electricity!'

And so he left the school of engineering and became an economist.

2 The Argument

Ivan Petrovich had an argument with his lady-friend, whom he kept trying to tell himself was 'the woman I love', but somehow it just wouldn't come out.

She was always trying to get something from him – it wasn't clear what – and was dissatisfied. Why was she dissatisfied? Ivan Petrovich did not know, nor did he feel like examining it in detail.

In the argument he upped and left her. Not that he felt indignant; he simply had to leave at that moment and the easiest way to do it was to arouse indignation in himself – and so he did. Slamming the door, he set his legs in motion down the stairs, quickly crossed the courtyard, and stopped at the street.

Oh, a deeply laid argument is such bliss! That's living with your lungs filled! But it must be hard for everyone to admit this, and it's not that admitting it is really useful, because some people may believe in it, and start having arguments again all too often – but let them remember that one shouldn't deliberately make things happen for oneself: besides, such a petty worry shouldn't interfere (which it often does anyway, unfortunately) with a man's sincere admissions about himself.

Here he was on the street again, or rather, he sensed that he was on the street – he had such a keen conception of it.

The parting sun was in its decline. Everything had begun to drift into a soft, deep blue.

Ivan Petrovich felt a touch of sadness in his body. He stood for a while and then sat down on a bench.

At this time of day, with the way the street is lit and its warm air, one can easily acquire a mood on a basis of sadness.

But he resisted. He stood up and started walking along the pavement on his listless legs. Beside him, on equally listless legs walked others, crossing the street at will, not at the corners. An uncrowded bus applied its brakes as it came upon them and moved along in jolts, and it was these jolts that were responsible for the stroll up and down the bus taken by two standing passengers.

There was no more sun but it was warm. He broke into a very fast walk in order to dislodge the warmth around him with air. For some reason the others also quickened their pace, but the air easily heated up against them and not only didn't make anyone the slightest bit cooler, but even worse.

At the corner where Ivan Petrovich always turned he noticed a window. Even before, it had always attracted his attention because it was very large and was always very noticeably shut tight.

Three sashes were now wide open in the outside casement, and in the inside casement as well; and in both casements the ventilation windows opened out, fitting one inside the other. It was suddenly apparent that the window had so many sashes, and now they were all opened wide for air – which in its warmth was in no way different from the homey, familiar air, but was nevertheless somehow better, more spacious perhaps.

Behind the window, in a room lit only from the street, in plain view, not hiding or arguing, was a small lively family of young people. The husband was busy at a table, turning the pages of something thick, but was not being overly pedantic. The behaviour of the woman was animated, pert. He understood that she was obviously more cheerful being next to a man like this – this husband – whom she had every right to slap on the back, grab by the shoulders, hit playfully about the neck, not knowing what else of this sort to do to him – and who would indulgently put up with it all.

Women (thought Ivan Petrovich) deal with the softest creatures – small children. But at the same time, they have to be on a level of understanding with their husbands, who for the most part have grown coarse with age, with work, or with wrong notions about life – which is what constitutes the duality of women. Both qualities always exist in them side by side, that is, softness and coarseness, flowing into each other and merging, and often showing through at an awkward time and scaring Ivan Petrovich.

'When they respond to a child and speak in their tender voice, sometimes even with a touch of sentimentality,' he thought, 'I expect them to turn around immediately with a retort if someone behind them says something coarse, as a husband might. They must indeed understand a very great deal in life (and take pleasure in their understanding), and in life, after all, we really mustn't be squeamish.

'There they are, all walking about with some direction, walking in twos, with men, or by themselves. How many of them I once knew! Not like now. And I was always very attracted by them. Many of them used to smile so sweetly at me and be so amiable when we talked, that I'd immediately get all worked up each time and my only thought would be: I'll choose my time and get to work, and then this one will be mine, and later another one. But the time somehow never came. Time slipped by rapidly: it was "today" – and then already it was "yesterday"; the girls kept settling down one after the other and carving out a life for themselves, and they no longer needed to smile at me when we met – and how sorry I was; my annoyance with myself and my hunger for those women I fell short of acquiring remained with me forever. There's no forgiving myself for this!

'And the way they walk! One step pulls a narrow skirt tight on a long thigh and then releases it slightly, shifting the wrinkles, and the next step tightens it again on the other thigh. After the leg is placed with the foot flat on the pavement, it remains astir for a long while, from the foot up to the knee; the knees rustle as they brush up against each other. No one step is like any other, it's either shorter or wider or to one side – not absolutely straight. It's the live walk of a live person, and it's a thrill to watch.

'And I'm going to have a look at every one of them,' thought Ivan Petrovich, upset by the argument. 'It'll be almost like touching them, even better, you can imagine more, and what's anyone going to say to me about it? Nothing. Not one of those men walking their girls, even if he guessed (from his own experience) – no one would do a thing to me, there's no reason to, he'd have no cause.'

He would never have discovered this for himself if it hadn't been for the argument, because it was shameful, because things like this are kept deeply hidden and suppressed. One mustn't even think of such things, he certainly knew that. But if you've had an argument and you give up on yourself, and if you are walking along the street and your arms are dangling, and your legs are moving nice and listlessly along the dark blue pavement – then, it's all right to.

3 Getting Acquainted

A trolleybus stopped next to Ivan Petrovich at a red light, and from force of habit he looked it over. There wasn't anyone standing in the bus since it wasn't crowded, and it seemed as if it were inhabited by heads. The heads were all looking out of the windows. Close by, right next to Ivan Petrovich, sat a girl who was staring at him through the glass. He kept her in sight only briefly, then let her go and started to look at the others. The others, however, were just ordinary people, whereas the girl's face immediately stuck in Ivan Petrovich's mind. It was a sort of ample face, with the kind of lines one would like to trace, one at a time, to the very end. He returned to the girl and wandered at length over her face with his eyes. The girl didn't find it unpleasant.

Suddenly Ivan Petrovich did not want the girl to just take off. The bus was standing there and might start up at any moment.

He began to smile at her a little sheepishly, because he had resolved to make her acquaintance come what may.

'Get off!', he mouthed and gestured at her. 'I (he pointed to himself) will be here, waiting, and you (he pointed to her) come here. All right?' (He nodded his head, encouraging her to nod back.)

'No,' she shook her head leisurely, but did not turn away – and if she were annoyed, she'd turn away, wouldn't she?

'All right, then, all right!' he said, starting to follow the bus, which had released its brakes and was about to move. 'Then let's do it another way (he crossed out his first option with both arms). You, you there (he gestured at her with his palm) – you'll get off over there and I'll run (he used his legs to show how he would run). All right? But wait for me! All right?'

How on earth he had managed to express everything he didn't know, but she had understood and felt that it was all right for her to do this; that is, that Ivan Petrovich was the kind of person whom it was all right, not dangerous, to get off and meet if she wanted to, because he would take it the right way. And she gave him a faint smile and nodded.

Ivan Petrovich broke into a run and overtook the bus, but it passed him again and the girl waved to him once more from the window.

And once again resentment welled up in him against women who are eager for perpetual close combat and insist upon being comforted, playing a game according to all the rules that someone once instilled in them. And suddenly he felt assurance (or rather, hope) that this time everything would be different, not like before. His long-cherished dream of one day meeting someone, a woman unlike the others only in this one respect, that she wouldn't insist upon combat – neither at the beginning of their acquaintance nor later would there be a struggle for supremacy, to see who is more important, to decide what you do her way and what you don't – this dream welled up in Ivan Petrovich, evoked by the street and the argument and the girl's highly unusual assent.

And here he was, running, running not very well, not beautifully or swiftly, not as he once did at the age of nineteen or
twenty (he had already turned thirty); and there she was, riding
ahead on a bus, a pretty girl with an unusual, ample face, and
she already trusted Ivan Petrovich more than the others had.

He did not even bother to prepare himself for the first words
of conversation, or possibly he didn't have time to, being lost
in his dream. But anyway the girl turned out to be rather bright:
she had worked out what to say so that they wouldn't feel
awkward at the beginning.

'Did you ever live in Pavlovsk? About six years ago?' she
asked Ivan Petrovich with an understanding smile.

'No,' he replied, with the same smile. 'Never!'

'Too bad,' she said. 'I guess I imagined it.'

'You must have,' Ivan Petrovich confirmed quickly and
cheerfully, because now it wasn't important. Now they could
get to know each other, since the beginning had gone so
smoothly.

Ivan Petrovich immediately began talking about himself –
where he lived, what he liked and didn't like, and she answered
in terms of herself, without waiting to be asked.

And they had one of those real conversations between two
people, when each one talks about himself and the other just
happens to find it interesting.

'I might not understand something right away,' said the girl
by way of example.

'Yes!' Ivan Petrovich concurred in amazement. 'I might not
either, right away!'

'But when I get home, I think about it and eventually I'll get
it. Then I start feeling ashamed.'

'Ashamed!' said Ivan Petrovich. 'No, most likely I would be
embarrassed, yes, that's it, most likely.'

'But *she* doesn't feel ashamed later on and *she* doesn't understand a thing even later on – now that's the main difference between her and me!'

'Yes!' Ivan Petrovich confirmed this difference and rejoiced
in it. 'Now take me, for example . . . If I . . .'

All the while, people wearing a variety of colours walked past
them along the avenue, out for a stroll. It was still rather
warm, and the somewhat younger fellows, not holding on to

their girls, as if not needing them, walked freely, one arm supported against their side and the other arm draping a jacket over the shoulder because of the heat. Whereas the ticket-collector felt hot and cramped in the trolleybus; as it went past, he was standing on the platform by the door, thrusting his middle-aged head into the city.

Ivan Petrovich attempted to take her by the arm – very gently, so he could immediately pretend it was an accident – but she did not shy away or object, and settled her elbow in his palm.

'If only I could come straight out with it,' thought Ivan Petrovich. 'If only I could come straight to the point.'

But Ivan Petrovich still could not make up his mind to do so.

Women possess something, like a particular product that everyone tries to obtain – feminine charm, a softness, perhaps – everything a woman is. At the same time, women have all the other human properties a man has, and they all think that someone the likes of Ivan Petrovich wants only that special thing from them, only that which is woman; as if, again, it were some kind of product. And the women who do not possess it feel sorrow and spite as a result; whereas the women who have it in abundance also feel resentful because they, on the other hand, think it's something that holds back the human being in them.

It's hard to say just how long they had been walking when Ivan Petrovich suddenly made up his mind.

'Shall we turn here?' Ivan Petrovich suggested cautiously. And they turned into a quiet street.

'I have a favourite side on every street,' said the girl. 'But not on this one. Should it be the right? – no, that's not my favourite. Should it be the left? – no, not the left, either. Which one *is* my favourite, then? Neither.'

'Let's kiss,' Ivan Petrovich urged all of a sudden, without any overture, stopping by a building.

'What?' said the girl, astonished. 'What did you say?'

'I really feel like kissing,' Ivan Petrovich said guiltily.

'Sure, sure, and there are a lot of things I'd like to do, too!' said the girl. 'You have to control yourself.'

'So she's already been struck by her unusual action – meeting someone on the street,' thought Ivan Petrovich, 'and she so clearly recognises this unusualness in herself, and she's so proud, that she's not up to continuing on the same tack with actions that are just as sincere as her first one.

'A game,' he said to himself with a sigh. 'They all have a need for us not to be straightforward with them and to submit to the rules of the game. But I don't want to. I want to be sincere! So then what?'

Ivan Petrovich knew, but didn't want to admit it to himself: he simply had to have in him the kind of game that would encompass her game, that's all there was to it – the way all young men have. But for him that game had finished.

'Well, this is where I live. Good-bye,' said the girl after they had made one more turn.

'Already?' exclaimed Ivan Petrovich. 'Well, all right, all right, I'll accompany you a little further!'

'But I'm already home. You don't have to accompany me any further. No one ever accompanies me any further – I don't allow it.'

'No, wait, I have to write down your phone number, don't I?' said Ivan Petrovich with cunning, in the way that one was supposed to do in this game, but also with annoyance. 'It's awkward here, let's go into the hallway.'

'Well, write it down,' said the girl as she went inside.

'What floor do you live on?' asked Ivan Petrovich, as one was supposed to in this situation.

'Why do you have to know?' said the girl (this, too, was customary).

'Just curious,' said Ivan Petrovich, ascending from one floor to the next. The girl meanwhile followed him up the stairs.

On the third floor Ivan Petrovich took her by the hand and pulled her to him.

'Who do you take me for?' the girl said rapidly, as if she had just been waiting for him to pull her to him.

'Wait a second, I didn't mean anything,' said Ivan Petrovich, putting his arm around her shoulder.

'Don't touch me, I don't let anyone touch me!'

'All right, I believe you, I can see you don't . . . But I'm not doing anything, am I? I'm not touching you.'

'We've only known each other for three hours. If it were three days at least . . . but three hours isn't enough.'

'But that's just a convention!' Ivan Petrovich cried out.

'People just decided on that, I mean that's what they agreed on. You and I can agree on something else.'

'No,' said the girl. 'We're not agreeing on anything else.'

'Why?' Ivan Petrovich said in despair, seizing her hands. 'Of course, I was waiting for you to say something like that. But let's give it a try, OK? Give it a try with me. I'm sure that it'll be the start of something for you and me. Let them all . . . do as they want, but we'll be different . . .'

'No,' she said, taking back her hands. 'There's not going to be any start. Don't you touch me! You're nice, sure, but what on earth are you saying? Just what do you think I am? I'm not that kind of girl!'

'No, no,' said Ivan Petrovich excitedly, 'of course you're not that kind of girl . . . well, I won't say a thing . . . I didn't think anything . . . you see . . . right now I . . .'

He carefully unfastened the two top buttons of her coat. She grasped his fingers and fastened her coat with her other hand. Ivan Petrovich noticed, however, that she had fastened only one button, the second. He then unfastened all four at once, the girl pushed him away, but then redid only two.

One by one he peeled these two last buttons from their holes and was left confronting a smooth, open-cut violet dress, but straight away he ran into the rigid edge of a palm jabbing him in his ribs.

'No!' said Ivan Petrovich with conviction. 'No, don't do that.'

'No, *I* say don't do that,' the girl replied.

'No-o . . . no, no . . . really, don't!' said Ivan Petrovich with even more conviction. 'Don't be that way with me, you really shouldn't, really!'

'Why should I give in to what you want? I said no, too, didn't I? So you give in to me!'

'I . . . all right, I'll give in . . . Generally, I . . .' said Ivan Petrovich, sliding his palms deeper and deeper under her coat, parting her from it. 'I'm not that kind . . . I mean I am that kind . . . I mean not in that sense . . . with me it's perfectly all right . . . with me this is the only way it should be . . .

'What did you do that for!' he suddenly cried out, taking offence as he distinctly felt a hand jamming into his ribs.

The girl was surprised and stopped, for the time being.

At last, he encircled her under her coat with both arms and bent her towards him – and she bent, fitting flush up against him. Now the rigid hand of opposition slackened, gave way, and dropped between them.

Ivan Petrovich was overcome with tenderness and trust.

They stood that way by a window, pressed against each other; or rather, the girl allowed him to press against her. He remained in that state of tenderness a little longer than necessary, and the girl was again surprised because she had already prepared herself for a continuation of the battle. When he at last began allowing his palms to stroke wherever they pleased, the girl's hands would seize them firmly, like gendarmes, on the outskirts of her dress – but no earlier – and promptly send them back again towards the centre, that is, towards the middle of the dress, to the waist.

The battle continued for a long time, with gradual surrenders and recaptures. Ivan Petrovich did not remember everything, he was only certain of the justness of his cause. He honestly knew that all of this was simply necessary – all that he was doing. And even vexation did not seriously get the better of him because the girl was gradually capitulating. Each time his hand made its way to the warm, living skin of her body, Ivan Petrovich shuddered with excitement, as if he had made his way to the naked, living, human essence of this girl, who was no longer concealed from him in her shell.

Suddenly someone started to come up the stairs. The girl sprang from his palms, quickly buttoned her coat, and turned towards the window.

Ivan Petrovich felt genuine sorrow.

An old woman carrying a long loaf of bread came up the stairs. She moved slowly, short of breath, taking rests by leaning on her knee with one hand. Her head gradually revolved around the stairwell until it reached them. Ivan Petrovich also began looking out of the window. They stood that way in silence, he and the girl, gazing out of the window as if there were something interesting going on. Two flies were crawling along the pane on either side, one over the other, turning from side to side in consonance, never a step apart, like friends.

After she had passed their landing, the old woman frequently stopped, looked at them from under her arm, and waited. On the sixth floor she fussed with her keys for a long while. Finally, she slammed the door and became quiet.

Ivan Petrovich instantly flung himself at the girl. He had to start all over again.

'No,' began the girl. 'That's enough, don't! . . . that's enough for today . . . We can't here.'

'Where then?' asked Ivan Petrovich with aspiration, as he set to work on the coat again.

'Nowhere,' she answered, but not very firmly. 'That's enough for today.'

'No!' Ivan Petrovich cried out. 'It so happens that's not enough for today! It can't be like that!'

'Yes, it can,' the girl said quickly.

'No,' said Ivan Petrovich, opening up the coat.

'Yes, it can . . .' the girl said once more and fell silent.

Under the coat everything was just as he had left it: everything unfastened was still unfastened; everything turned back remained turned back. As a result, Ivan Petrovich was overcome again, and he rushed to kiss and stroke the girl's body, and she retreated a bit more rapidly than before.

They were already so entangled that sometimes as he kissed downwards somewhere at her body, Ivan Petrovich would land on himself and kiss his own shoulder or arm by mistake and notice it only afterwards.

Unexpectedly, the girl flung her forearms over Ivan Petrovich's shoulders, raised herself a little higher and pressed herself against him tightly. She no longer had any room to retreat.

Weakly but insistently Ivan Petrovich forced her to step backwards slightly. She gave way and they suddenly took that step in unison and came into contact with the wall . . .

And at last there it all was.

They stood there then for a short while, holding each other tightly. The girl, stunned, went off to her apartment, while Ivan Petrovich, bearing her phone number, made his way downstairs to the exit.

He emerged from the front door as if he were thoroughly cleansed inside and out, good, fresh. The street had become dark and spacious. The long day of his dependence – so offensive to him – was over. The close combat foisted upon him he had won.

But now he thought: just who was the victor? He may have won the battle, yet the battle *had* taken place. Isn't that what they were after – all those who wanted him to take part in that sort of close combat? It was clear that in any event the victory was by right his. He was the man, it was all consistent with the laws, in accord with nature. And he – too weak as he was to change everything – all he had managed to do was hasten the victory and shorten the length of battle. Even that was hard – it had taken him a whole day. True, it might have been a month or a year, or even longer. Well, anyway, he had been slightly victorious, hadn't he? But only very slightly, just barely.

This game, with its laws, its ploys – women themselves had accustomed him to it (why did they have to do it?). And what's worse, he was well aware that if he were sincere with them in this, sincerity too would fit perfectly into the game; the game works – you couldn't think of any better system no matter how hard you tried.

In other words, he should stay away from all women, then single out one of them and check her very carefully. But how should he single one out? What if he didn't find her?

'No,' Ivan Petrovich said to himself with unexpected force, becoming indignant. 'A man just mustn't be so unbearably cautious about all this, as if a certain part of his organism weren't verging on freedom, lightly held in place by four buttons through which the wind can frolic, but instead were located in some far-away office to be doled out, like a loan, under the strict control of the whole state.'

'Lord!' said Ivan Petrovich, not addressing God, whom he did not know, but simply because he was used to this short sob-like word: 'What happiness people have been given between their legs! And what they do with it! How unforgivably badly they treat it!'

And here another thing suddenly revealed itself to Ivan Petrovich: all the close combat, all the ploys of the game – women didn't think all that up by themselves! The powers-that-be ordered them to act that way; through them, through women, the powers-that-be exert influence on a man, when at last they release him at the sound of a bell. Through women they command their men, they dispatch a woman to him already brought up to suit his needs, already instructed, from a very early age, instructed in her mother's belly, instructed by generations, by centuries — how can you hold out against them?

To a woman, of course, it seems that she's doing just as she likes. But in actual fact, that's not been the case at all. Even when she kisses you, she's been allowed to kiss you, she's been thrust upon you for kisses, let loose — it's as if through her lips you are being reluctantly kissed by the consenting powers.

All in all, Ivan Petrovich once again felt hurt by some higher authority.

Part Two

DUSYA

'If two people huddle together, that's God already; it's as simple as that.'

— *From an old diary.*

1 Dusya's Money

I

This time Dusya's vacation was in the winter. She didn't go to visit her mother – it was a long way, cost money, and she hadn't put any away. There wasn't anything to put it away from; she had not earned much, and besides, she had started sending some to her mother because she knew from her mother's letters that it would come in handy. They would have plenty of opportunities to see one another.

Dusya had worked out an agreement with an old retired woman in the suburbs and there she spent her vacation, her two weeks, on a shoestring.

The old lady didn't keep track of dates, she didn't really care what day it was, especially since her pension was delivered to her at home and she couldn't bear waiting until the next remittance anyway – so it was no use even counting the days.

So in the end Dusya was late getting back to work after the vacation because she got the days mixed up.

'I was two days late for work,' she wrote in her note of explanation, 'because while I was on vacation, I didn't keep up with tearing the days off the calendar and got mixed up about what date it was. Please punish me to the full extent of Soviet law.'

She was punished, but not as she feared, not to the full legal extent: she was simply given a reprimand on the factory bulletin board. There was only one bad thing – a reprimand entailed a mandatory loss of bonus, and the following month she received only her basic pay, that is, twenty rubles less than usual.

'Never mind,' thought Dusya. 'I'll set things straight somehow, little by little.'

For the time being, however, not only couldn't she straighten herself out, but even worse. Because, on top of everything else, Dusya was put to much shame by her forewoman for being late. She still thought that Dusya had blatantly lied to her, and gradually Dusya really did feel ashamed. Sometimes she would feel ashamed and not fulfil her quota, in spite of the poster that hung in front of her nose: 'Our motto is – the quota is within the reach of everyone!'

II

That day Dusya suddenly seemed to become a little more grown-up, and right before the end of her shift the last wart on her finger fell off.

'I didn't fulfil my quota again today,' said Dusya, returning to her dormitory after work. 'How much money will I make again? What a laugh! And my forewoman gives me hell, too. Is it my fault?'

'I didn't meet my quota for two years and only began to later on,' responded Lyuba.

'Dusya, there's a package for you from your mum,' said Nina. 'Look!'

'Oh, let's see,' said Dusya. 'Oh yes – it's probably eggs. The hens are laying well at the moment.'

Without delay, Dusya went downstairs and walked over to the post office. Inside the package, sure enough, there turned out to be two dozen eggs.

'And share them with your boyfriend, I don't mind,' Dusya's mother wrote her in a letter enclosed in the package so she wouldn't have to pay extra for it. 'You must have a boyfriend, even though you won't write to your mother about him. The flooding this spring was bad, the water came up to the lilacs and seeped behind the shrubs into the back cellar. Three huge slabs of ice were left in the vegetable garden and lay there all summer, especially one, until it turned into long needles and finally melted. The shed has started to tip and needs fixing. They charge so much nowadays, I don't know what to do. Ilya Margyunov came by and he says, "Don't you go asking anyone, granny, I'll do it for you in no time, granny." He and his granny this and granny that, but he'll gladly make you pay through the nose. You know that Ilya.'

'Greetings, dear mama!' wrote Dusya in reply. 'Thanks for the eggs. They arrived safely. Only two got broken in the mail, but I put them in the frying pan immediately, and they never had a chance to leak, except for a tiny bit of the white. Have the shed fixed, I'm sending you a money order separately for as much as I can. As far as Ilya Margyunov is concerned, offer him half a pint, don't offer him any more to start with. Then later on tell him I promise him another pint. Then he won't make you pay through the nose and he'll fix it faster, because whatever he screws you out of goes to his wife, he can't lie to her, he doesn't know how to, I know. He'll be afraid that people won't let him get away with it. A pint right under his nose will be much more appealing. For the time being I don't have a boyfriend and there's no need, he wouldn't be of any use to me right now. So the girls and I will eat the eggs ourselves. They always share with me too if they have something. And so for now I give you a big, big kiss. Your daughter, Dusya.'

Dusya sealed the letter with her tongue and took it down to the mailbox across from her building.

Alongside the mailbox, on a bench, sat a man wearing a jacket bulging at the pockets. He beckoned to Dusya with a long finger.

'Excuse me just a minute,' the man said without commas.

And there he sat, bulging; a wisp of cloth peeped through a tear in the shoulder of his jacket.

'Now what in heaven's name does he want?' thought Dusya, but she was curious and walked over to him.

'Little lady!' he addressed her, and Dusya found this form of address pleasing.

'I am very, very, very, very — ASHAMED!' he said loudly but not at all ashamedly. Dusya wanted to laugh but she didn't.

'If the union had given me sick pay, I never would have been so bold as to offer you . . . here . . .' He began pulling shiny cans from his pockets. 'One . . . three . . . four . . . if the union had

given me sick pay ... here, look, little lady, canned pork ...
I'm offering it to you cheap, the supplies of a better life, half a
ruble apiece. Let me repeat: I am very, very, very, very
ASHAMED!'

The last word he intoned menacingly, as he continued pulling
out can after can; it was puzzling how he had got them all in.

'Poor man,' thought Dusya with a feeling of sympathy for the
latter word. 'Nothing to buy a drink with. And I could use
them. I'll send them to mum. Meat is really scarce there now.
I'm broke – never mind, I'll borrow some. And I'll keep two
cans for myself, and now I've got eggs, I'll boil some potatoes,
there's still enough tea left for a pot – now that's breakfast and
dinner for three days. And canned pork costs almost twice as
much in the store. Look at all the advantages! And later on we'll
see.'

Nothing would be seen, but no matter.

'Hold on a minute, friend,' said Dusya. 'I'll go and get the
money. You won't leave, now?'

'I can't wait long,' the man replied. 'But I'll wait for you. Go
and get your money, miss.'

He seated himself with his knees spread apart, his spine
arched against the back of the bench, and his arms stretched
out as wide as possible – in this uncomfortable position he
evidently felt a considerable degree of freedom.

But he soon became tired from his freedom, from his auto-
nomy, from his independence of the bends of the bench. He
seated himself normally.

'Girls, give me five rubles. Who can I borrow from until I
get my advance?' said Dusya, running into the room.

'I'm all out,' replied Lyuba.

'What do you need it for?' asked Nina.

Here she should have explained it, but she didn't.

'I need it. I'll tell you later. You mean nobody has any
money? I really need it!'

'Wait a sec,' said Nina. 'I'll try to come up with something.'

She looked in her purse, at first only on top, and then deeper.
She sat with it open wide in her hands in front of her and whispered something. She fished out a five-ruble note, then stuffed
it back in. She made a mental calculation, then suddenly figured
it out.

'Okay, here, take it, I'll survive somehow.'

'Thanks a million!' Dusya rejoiced and grabbed the note. 'I'll pay you back! Maybe even sooner!' she shouted from the doorway, and dashed off.

Sure enough, the man was still waiting. He had piled the cans on the bench and covered them up with the bottom edge of his jacket, like a brooding hen.

'There, you see, under cover,' he said in a flutter. 'Everything as it should be. I feel very, very, very . . .' he began again but became pensive and forgot to finish.

Dusya politely folded the note lengthwise and, pinching it in her fingers, she handed it over tactfully. She gathered the cans into a string bag and ran home.

Without telling anyone, she opened one of the cans in the kitchen. A profuse thin liquid came spurting out of the hole.

'Juicy,' thought Dusya, 'that's good.'

Instead of pork, the can contained green peas.

'He got it mixed up!' Dusya feared for the man. 'Why, that idiot got the cans mixed up!'

She tried to imagine – what will he do when he finds out? – and even hoped he might never notice.

But as it turned out – no, he hadn't mixed them up, he hadn't made a mistake. There were green peas in all the cans.

'Looks like he cheated me!' Dusya suddenly realised with incomprehensible joy. 'And he cheated me so well, so politely! Well, it's my own fault. So what of it, it's nothing,' Dusya calmed herself down as if she were someone else. 'I can eat peas too, instead of breakfast. To be honest, I even like peas. It's nothing, it could have been even worse.'

It couldn't have been worse because now there was no way of getting any money, not from anywhere, and soon she'd have to pay it back. Dusya had already borrowed from everyone in her room; they themselves didn't have any more and wouldn't have. 'Everything we've got,' as the saying goes, 'but money, sorry to say, we no got. Where can we get it? It doesn't grow on trees. That's why we don't have any.'

'Actually, I don't really need any,' thought Dusya. 'It would just be nice to get out of this mess, but then again, what's the use? There's no getting out of it now. Never!'

Dusya sat alone for a while in the dark kitchen, and then went back to her room for some sympathy. Only Katya and Nina were there.

'You idiot! My, are you an idiot!' said Katya, with all the anger she could muster.

'You might have at least asked us, at least dropped a hint,' said Nina, getting upset.

'Katya, Nina,' Dusya suddenly said distinctly. 'I spilled the salt today.'

'So?' said Katya in amazement.

'Katya, let's not argue. We argue and we think it's us, but it's only the salt. Let's not give it the satisfaction.'

Here she sat down on the bed, turned away, and cried for a moment – moistly, but without sound.

Lyuba came back and turned on the radio.

'And now the weather,' it said. And that's all it had time to say. Dusya rushed over and switched it off and would not listen to it any longer. She did not expect anything good from the weather.

'What's up with you?' Lyuba said in amazement. They told her.

'No, I'll just have to go out on the street, I guess,' Dusya said unexpectedly with force, wiping away her lament.

These words did not disappear as usual to where they always disappear. They remained hanging in the room, somewhere beneath the lamp with the lilac shade.

'You're kidding, Dusya, think what you're saying,' Katya said, very quickly, as if she had been thinking about it herself.

'Why save it?' said Lyuba. 'We save it and save it – and for what? A good man doesn't give a damn about it, and I sure don't want to save it for a bad one.'

'You don't have anything to save any more, anyway,' Nina said with severity. 'It was snatched from you.'

'I gave it away myself. Didn't come cheap,' Lyuba said, louder than necessary, and went out to the kitchen.

Everyone else quietened down.

'Yes,' Nina all at once said seriously. 'It's obvious you'll have to make a little trip to the street. If I had any money I'd give it to you right away, even ten rubles. But I'm nearly broke myself.'

'Once you get out of debt things will take care of themselves,' Katya also agreed.

'Take Marusya Lopukhova. You know Marusya Lopukhova?'

'No,' Dusya replied.

'What do you mean, of course you know Marusya, in our shop, she's sort of . . . well, you know.'

Nina drew a circular outline in the air with both hands, spreading them wider and wider.

'Oh, her,' said Dusya. 'Yes, I know her.'

'Well, she went once. She got everything straightened out right away and even started saving for a coat. She's been saving for a year already and she'll probably get it pretty soon. Of course, she's got looks, not like you.'

'Aren't you scared?' asked Katya with interest.

'No, I'm not scared,' Dusya answered. 'It doesn't bother me, it's only this once. It can't be helped, if that's how it's got to be.'

'Yes,' said Katya. 'There's nothing else you can do. If you want to make it quick, that's how you can make it.'

'No, you can't earn a lot all at once nowadays,' Nina asserted knowingly. 'You can't. All part-time jobs on the side have been cut or else pay peanuts.'

And Dusya went off to the main street.

2 *Ashamed*

All day long Ivan Petrovich had not thought about women.

But by the evening he just couldn't resist it any longer and he started thinking.

At first he remembered the girl from yesterday, but he was immediately overwhelmed by a surge of resentment.

Of course the girl was waiting for him to call her. She felt that *now* he was already obliged to call her. The conviction that her behaviour with him had been sacrificial, unusual, was already securely ensconced in her. What, just what had she sacrificed for Ivan Petrovich? What could she, as a matter of fact, give away to him? Only the woman that she contained and no more, and that was very little. But look how much has gone into the setup, how much degrading dependence he's supposed to feel with her, how he is made to yield even if he doesn't feel like yielding; how he is made to attack, even if he had never in his life liked to attack.

'No,' Ivan Petrovich said to himself, becoming frightened. 'I'm not going to call that girl today. I'm not going to call anyone today.

'Women?' thought Ivan Petrovich, trying to summon up indifference. 'There's no need, don't bother, I already know in advance everything that'll happen.

'I mean there's no need to invite them or take them somewhere, or to try and persuade them to do something – or put your arms around them, that is,' quickly correcting himself for fairness' sake. 'As it is, all the women around me, all those walking by, all those I come upon, those who live near me for some reason or other – I immediately have them right there in my heart!'

By this manner of thinking he sharpened his acute resentment towards women, until it had a keen edge. Then he got ready, went downstairs, walked out of his building, paced up and down in front of the entrance, turned into a side-street, walked down the side-street, came out onto a main road and then onto an avenue, grasped the ends of his sleeves with his fingers, and slowly let his eyes roam promiscuously.

People were coming from all directions onto the avenue. They hurried, ran, crushed together in a trolleybus, leaped onto a bus, changed to another, and when they finally reached the avenue, instantly calmed down, straightened themselves up, and set out for a walk – arms alongside their bodies, one foot after the other, in no hurry.

'What pleasure I get simply from my own eyes!' said Ivan Petrovich in wonder, and he even touched his eyes with one finger. They protruded under the lids and trembled slightly, in a hurry to open up as soon as the finger was taken away. 'How tenaciously they latch onto everything in their path! Most of all, of course, I like people: the way they walk, the way they look and dress. But then again, it's the women that I find the more interesting.'

Here, look, just youngsters – hardly any breasts. The way they pace, strut in formation, lightly tossing about the hems of their dresses with their legs!

There's a calm, mature woman standing in front of a store. She hasn't protected her knees with her dress, doesn't need to;

while *he*, standing next to her, leans over and writes an address in his cupped hand.

Three young fellows are making a concerted effort to talk a red-headed girl into something, while nearby, a little to the side, standing out of the way, are two other girls, already irrevocably persuaded, calmly waiting without interfering.

A very tall girl is walking around town at night all alone, completely unafraid. Who in the world would make a play for her? Not just anyone. No one is going to turn up who could make a play for her, or even reach her shoulder.

Ivan Petrovich watched with his mouth open. 'How could you embrace her?' he thought. 'How do they embrace such huge women?'

A gramophone set at the wrong speed, too fast for the record, blared out of a window in a churring asexual voice.

Even on trolleybuses Ivan Petrovich would always find a woman's face that could suit him – that is, one with which a connection might be established within him – and he would rest against that face with his eyes, expecting no response from it. 'Why is that?' he would sometimes think.

Suddenly Ivan Petrovich stood still. A pretty girl in slacks swaggered past him. Instantly he pinned his eyes to her.

No, she wasn't one of those slender-limbed girls who have been extracted from ordinary clothes and transplanted into a pair of men's trousers; this was a grenadier in bright, grey buckskins tightly filled with everything that ought to fill them, with recesses marked wherever they should be, the lines of the buttocks delicate, the red boots stylish, coming up to the swelling of the calf.

'Just look at that!' Ivan Petrovich exclaimed to himself. 'What people there are walking around here these days! Phenomenal people.

'Ah, what pleasure comes to me through my eyes!' he marvelled once again and narrowed his eyes for an instant. 'There goes a man whose body is overgrown along the sides and from the belly; as he walks he puts his weight on his right leg. I get pleasure from him too, because I can see how stupendously overgrown he is, how earnestly he applies his weight. I think it's dishonest! People walk along still, unaware that my eye is getting pleasure from them. Maybe they'd do something if they knew? Hide their bellies, rumple their clothes, not stride, not wink, not write in cupped hands.

'No, it really is shameful,' said Ivan Petrovich almost loudly, and he actually did feel ashamed.

3 Completely Ashamed

'Here I am, walking along the street modestly,' thought Ivan Petrovich (and now he really was walking very modestly), 'I'm not scrutinising any more of the women, I'm not brazenly making a play for them like others, and they should all appreciate this; they themselves! They should like me for this – for my modesty, which others don't have – in spite of my desire to get to know them, women, that is.

'But they've got to appreciate the restraint that's in me; they mustn't think that I'm simply preoccupied, don't even want to look at them, that there's simply nothing in me to hold back from them – they certainly wouldn't like that about me!'

Ivan Petrovich started to get upset, started to glance around, and saw a girl walking towards him slowly, strangely, as though towards something already accomplished, already settled, looking at him with wide-open eyes.

She too was walking unconstrainedly and, as it seemed to Ivan Petrovich, somewhat sadly along the pavement, on straight legs, wearing a fluid silky top not quite in keeping with the weather. Her rounded arms dangled by her body along her fine, solid frame. Her hair hung over her ears in a square cut, falling from her ears onto her face. Her face evidently wasn't accustomed to being made to look attractive – otherwise it might have been pretty.

'I'd move that hair away from her face,' suddenly passed through Ivan Petrovich's mind.

'Take me with you!' he said, surprising himself. He said it casually and was about to walk on.

The girl stopped, looked him over, and uttered with a sigh: 'Oh, all right.'

'So . . . shall we go then?' said Ivan Petrovich, flustered.

'Fine,' replied Dusya. 'Only, you'll have to pay me some money.'

'Oh, you're that kind of girl . . .' said Ivan Petrovich, a little frightened.

'Yes,' Dusya confirmed. 'I'm that kind.'

'You mean they're still around now?' said Ivan Petrovich in amazement.

'Of course,' said Dusya. 'Here I am, after all.'

'All right, then,' said Ivan Petrovich after a moment's thought. 'I'm willing. Where shall we go?'

'Where were you inviting me to?'

'Well, I was just . . . I didn't know . . . well, to the movies or wherever people generally go now. To a restaurant.'

'No, I don't go to restaurants,' said Dusya with alarm. 'I've never even been to a restaurant. I mean my dates have very often invited me and even tried to make me go, but I wouldn't go. I didn't want to settle up with them afterwards.'

'What do you mean "settle up"?' asked Ivan Petrovich.

'I never liked owing anything. Even if someone pays for my ticket to the movies, I'll discreetly pay him back another time. But a restaurant costs so much money all at once – it would take me a week to earn that much! I really don't have the heart to spend all that money at one go, and I don't think he does either, but he goes ahead and spends it anyway. So then, he's probably counting on something. I'm supposed to pay him back, but I don't want to. So I've never gone because I've never been able to bring myself to settle up.'

'Wait a minute, wait a minute,' said Ivan Petrovich, and he began blinking in confusion. 'You have to settle up afterwards, since you're that kind of girl, right? Or aren't you that kind? I don't get it.'

'No, no,' Dusya assured him. 'I am, only I don't want a restaurant in return.'

'But anyway, wouldn't you like to go to a restaurant? Aren't you interested?'

'Well, of course I'm interested, I've never been to one. I am interested, but not very. I've been invited very often, but I never went. Maybe that's why I was invited – because I wouldn't go. Look at Valya, she's dying to be invited, but they don't ask her because she'd like to. And so I say: "Valya will go with you; you go with them, Valya!". "They're not asking me," Valya says, "they're asking you." And she gets offended. And sure enough, they don't ask her, while me they invite and try hard to get me to go – and all because I won't go.'

'Then where else?' Ivan Petrovich struggled. 'I'd still like to go to a restaurant, how about it?'

'Why a restaurant, for heaven's sake?' Dusya said in amazement and slyly gave Ivan Petrovich the once-over. 'That's not what you want, is it?'

'No,' Ivan Petrovich replied, after a little thought.

'How can we do "that" in a restaurant?'

'We can't,' Ivan Petrovich agreed.

'Can't we at your place?' asked Dusya.

'At my place . . .' Ivan Petrovich stopped short. 'No. We can't at my place.'

Ivan Petrovich could not bring himself to that.

'I'm really very quiet, don't you worry. I can even tidy up at your place, if you live alone. And if you're worried about the neighbours, never mind, you can slip me in, we'll be so quiet (I really can be!) that no one will notice. And I won't leave the room at all; I don't even have to go to the lavatory. I can hold it in for a very long time, really and truly.'

'No,' Ivan Petrovich said with difficulty, blushing. 'I'm not alone.'

It wasn't true.

'Well, we'll have to go to my place then,' said Dusya regretfully. 'What can you do.'

And off they went to the dormitory.

4 The Dormitory

In the room there were four beds, a table, chairs, and a wardrobe. It was an ordinary room, like any other in any dormitory, slightly adapted for unpretentious communal living.

As always, the beds, the table, the chairs, the wardrobe, and especially the walls showed signs of attention bestowed by the girls living in their midst, and bore traces of their efforts to create a little beauty around them, reflecting their taste and their means.

Pillows stood upright, balanced on one corner, in the middle of each bed. The table was covered with an openwork cotton cloth. Between the wall and the wardrobe were fixed plywood shelves on which spare shoes were kept. The shelves were painted pink, and movie stars were glued to the one on top.

The principal decoration on the walls was the tear-off calendar – three whole calendars for different years. Nothing had been torn from the calendars in any of these years, but they were nicely swollen and accordioned away from the wall at the bottom, evidently because they were read frequently.

It wasn't just any calendar, by the way; it was a calendar made specially for women, and the girls enjoyed leafing through its pages every day, particularly Katya.

Every morning, when she awoke from sleep, she turned back the outdated pages and found the new, current day.

'What do we have today?' Katya would say to herself. 'Let's have a look.'

And she would look.

' "How are you, fellow countrymen of steel? . . ." read Katya. 'No . . . that was yesterday. Today . . . where is today? Ah, here we are: "In the world of capitalism sixty per cent of the population starve annually." (Imagine that! How awful! They're starving!)'

'Where's that, where?' asked Nina.

'In America, I said, under capitalism!'

'You mean such a high percentage all at once? Does it really say that?'

'That's what it says,' said Katya. 'And how would you know about it if it weren't for the calendar?'

And everyone agreed, sure enough, they would never have known.

'What did it say a year ago today? Let's look,' Katya would say to herself.

And she'd look.

' "Gymnastic exercises for middle-aged women." It's too bad I'm not middle-aged yet. But someday I will be. That means some day these exercises will come in handy.'

'Now I know everything that a person has to know these days,' Katya often said. 'And it's all thanks to the calendar.'

And that was true.

The door of their room had been painted white on the inside

but the outside was still green. Dusya knocked first, as if she were a stranger, and only then opened it.

'Well now, let me introduce you,' said Dusya, as she walked in with Ivan Petrovich.

'Hi,' said Ivan Petrovich, embarrassed, and shook his head in the direction of two walls.

The girls all said hello and told him their names.

'Here's some money,' said Ivan Petrovich. 'Please get some wine and snacks.'

'All right,' said Dusya, getting her purse. She shook the purse and fumbled around in it with her hands.

'I still say I don't like my purse,' she said upon reflection. 'First of all, because it's often empty.'

'And second?' asked Ivan Petrovich.

'What?' Dusya repeated the question. 'Second?'

Again she reflected.

'In the second place, for the same reason.'

Dusya took the money from Ivan Petrovich and left.

'Now don't you get bored,' she said, turning back from her errand. 'Girls, don't you let him get bored, OK?'

And she departed.

Ivan Petrovich sat down and smiled a little to start things off.

'O Krivorozhe, my Krivorozhe,' crooned the radio.

The girls were sitting on their beds and they all looked rather alike to Ivan Petrovich. Such nice girls, obviously jolly, but maybe not.

'Krivorozhe, you're the sweetest town in the world,' the radio sang joyously.

Katya was kneeling on her bed and leafing through the calender.

'What are you looking for?' asked Nina.

'Nothing special,' Katya replied. 'They say that in America they've invented a machine that can tell if a person is lying. They put something on you and plug something in, and they immediately know if you're telling the truth or not. Is that right?'

'Yes,' confirmed Ivan Petrovich, pleased that he didn't have to remain silent. 'That's right, there is such a machine.'

'There really is?' Nina said in astonishment.

'What they ought to do,' said Lyuba with some ulterior motive, 'is to run all men through that machine.'

'Yeah,' said Katya. 'Wouldn't it be great to find out what they're really thinking!'

'Why men?' asked Ivan Petrovich, slightly offended. 'If someone's lying, he's lying. So what's the difference if it's a man or a woman?'

'A woman doesn't lie to a man,' Nina said harshly. 'And if she does lie, it's because that's what he wants. But a man deceives a woman all the time.'

'Even if he's just having a conversation with her he lies,' added Nina. 'Why is it he pretends to be modest with a woman, but with other men how does he talk? You know perfectly well. Men can only talk crudely to each other.'

'Yeah,' said Lyuba. 'I feel that way, too. When I'm in male company, I'm always afraid they'll forget and say something they shouldn't. And even though I could tell them a thing or two myself, I'm still somehow afraid of their conversations.'

'We don't particularly believe you, either, keep that in mind,' said Nina. 'You said your name was Vanya, but we didn't really believe that very much. Right?'

'Right,' replied Katya. 'Maybe you're not Vanya.'

'But why on earth would I want to lie? Does it really make any difference?' Ivan Petrovich smiled, as if at a joke, trying not to appear ill at ease.

'Who knows what advantage you might get from it,' Nina said severely. 'A man always lies a little to a woman.'

'Well, in our country everybody is equal,' said Ivan Petrovich, not wanting to argue.

'What's that? Everybody is equal?' repeated Nina.

'Of course,' Ivan Petrovich blithely confirmed.

'Yeah, and you're equal to yourself,' Katya said reproachfully, as though to a child. 'Do you seriously believe that?'

Ivan Petrovich grew thoughtful. Why not, why not seriously?

'That's right, everybody's equal in our country,' he said again, smiling and wishing to show that he wasn't given to arguing, but that he was a normal, nice guy without any ulterior motives.

'You mean men and women?' asked Nina.

'Well, not only . . . By and large, everybody is equal.'

'Yes, of course they are . . .' Katya began, but was immediately interrupted by Nina:

'Let me say something.'

She was silent for a moment, as if trying to think of the simplest way of explaining it to Ivan Petrovich, and then said distinctly, feigning agreement with him:

'Well, all right, everybody *is* equal. Then why is a general still fatter than, say, a colonel?'

'Yes!' Katya jumped up. 'Why?'

'And why is a colonel always twice as fat as an ordinary lieutenant?'

'Come on, tell us why!' Katya rejoiced.

'It's true, I once went out with a lieutenant. He was very skinny,' Lyuba confirmed.

'And they're all fatter than the rank and file. Quite a bit, as a matter of fact!' Nina concluded firmly.

'Well, why is it, then?' asked Katya, looking straight at Ivan Petrovich.

'I wonder why too sometimes,' said Lyuba somewhat less solemnly, unlike the others.

Everyone waited to hear what Ivan Petrovich would say to this.

Just then the door opened and in walked Dusya with her purchases.

'Not bored, I hope?' she asked in a voice totally different from the one in which everyone in the room had just been speaking.

'No,' Ivan Petrovich said honestly. 'I'm not bored.'

And he sighed.

Dusya was calm and even cheery. Her shopping had gone quickly in spite of the queue, and she felt good about it. And because her diet had been meagre recently, it was clear and bright in her stomach, and it was easy to imagine how things were stacked up in there. And this also made her thoughts run clear. Dusya had even sung softly on the way.

'Let's never quarrel . . .' she sang. Dusya liked this song for its underlying idea.

'Let's ne-e-ver quarrel!' She couldn't remember any more of the words and so sang like this: tya-ra-ra.

In her bag she had brought home a pint bottle of vodka, half a pound of sausages, and a quarter of a pound of butter.

'Why so little?' asked Ivan Petrovich.

And Dusya replied: 'It's enough.'

She collected the change in her purse and her pockets and laid it all in front of Ivan Petrovich. Ivan Petrovich was surprised and put it away.

'Well, how about it?' he said indecisively. 'Come on . . . Katya, Nina . . . Lyuba . . . Come on, Dusya, let's have a little drink. Only, what's there to drink here? No, this isn't enough, just not enough! We've got money! It just so happens that today was my payday.'

'I don't want any,' replied Nina. 'Thank you.'

'Neither do I,' said Katya. 'Thanks, anyway.'

'You have a drink,' said Dusya. 'It'll improve your frame of mind. We girls don't need to, we're all cheery as it is.'

'No, I wouldn't mind a sip,' said Lyuba. 'Just one!'

'That's it, that's it,' Ivan Petrovich rejoiced. 'That's what I say, too!'

'Lyuba,' said Nina. 'What's the matter with you, never had a drink before? Cut it out!'

'All right,' said Dusya, making the decision as though in charge. 'Go to the store yourself, then, Lyuba, OK? Buy a bottle of port and a small loaf of bread – I forgot. Don't spend any more than that, though, there's no need to. It doesn't grow in his purse, either.'

'I'll be back in no time!' Lyuba shouted and ran off.

She returned with the wine before they had even had time to start talking again.

She poured the change into Dusya's palm; Dusya counted it and returned it to Ivan Petrovich.

They all drank ceremoniously, having one apiece; they didn't bother to sit around the table. Then all except Dusya and Ivan Petrovich immediately dispersed and sat down on their own beds.

'Whatever am I doing?' Ivan Petrovich suddenly thought, and took a clear look at Dusya. 'I've got to get out of here right away!'

'All right, then,' Dusya said to Ivan Petrovich. 'Had your drink? Had something to eat?'

'Yes,' replied Ivan Petrovich. 'I have.'

'Let's turn the light out now,' said Dusya. 'Girls, OK if I turn out the light?'

'Go ahead,' said Nina.

'Sure, it's time for bed,' Katya agreed.

Lyuba laughed to herself for some reason and told herself something funny: 'You're walking along and someone yells out, "Why are you walking with your heels backwards?" You look, and they really are backwards. What a laugh!'

She laughed at herself again and began unbuttoning her blouse ready for bed.

'If I leave, they'll think I'm being mean,' Ivan Petrovich said to himself.

Meanwhile, the light was put out.

'Now I won't even be able to find the way out,' he thought. There was no alternative but to get into bed with Dusya.

'Now it's too late for anything else,' he thought. 'Well, all right, let whatever happens happen!

'But she won't be any the worse for it, after all! There's nothing bad about it, in itself it's a fine thing,' he thought honestly. 'Maybe with someone else it would be bad, but it can't be bad for her with me, with me it can't be bad for anybody. I'll take it all the right way, after all, and that's the most important thing. There's no telling whom she might be with and it's better with me anyway, I'm the sort of person ...' Ivan Petrovich did not define what sort of person he was, but he felt it inside and tried to convey it to Dusya.

'Just keep in mind that I'm a virgin,' said Dusya.

'By morning we'll know, we'll know everything,' Ivan Petrovich hurriedly began nodding into the darkness.

'No, it's true,' Dusya said stubbornly.

'What can we do about it now?' Ivan Petrovich responded rapidly, not allowing himself to become frightened. 'It doesn't matter any more now whether you're a virgin or not.'

'No, it's the truth, just keep that in mind. Lyuba, I really am a virgin, aren't I?'

'Yes,' replied Lyuba. 'She really is a virgin, take my word for it.'

'Katya, am I a virgin?'

'Yes,' replied Katya. 'You're a virgin.'

'All of us here are virgins, except Lyuba,' said Nina, setting her alarm clock by touch.

'I know, it's harder with a virgin, but that's all right, do your best, just keep it in mind, that's all,' said Dusya.

On all sides everyone had grown still.

Lyuba lay there, recalling her lieutenant.

'What am I to do when I want to?' he had said to her several times before it happened.

'And really, what is he supposed to do when he feels like it?' thought Lyuba. 'Go gallivanting after others, maybe?'

And she had given in.

'But promise me something, then it'll be easier for me,' she had asked.

'No, I can't promise anything. Now's not the time to make you a promise,' he'd answered bluntly.

'What can you do?' thought Lyuba without the least bit of sadness.

Elsewhere in the dormitory people were getting ready to go to sleep – moving about, snorting, washing. Doors whined like little children.

'Not right away,' Dusya suddenly said in a loud whisper. 'Even a pigeon doesn't mount his mate until he's done enough billing and cooing; otherwise she won't let him.'

'That's really true!' Ivan Petrovich thought in amazement.

He made a long and diligent effort to cover Dusya with his corner of the blanket, becoming entangled himself.

'Not that way,' said Dusya, and she straightened out the blanket properly.

'Oh yes, of course,' said Ivan Petrovich.

Steps travelled up and down the staircase.

'The bed creaks,' Ivan Petrovich voiced quietly a little later.

'So what?' asked Dusya. 'Does it bother you?'

'No, of course not, don't be silly,' replied Ivan Petrovich. 'It's just awkward. We're making it hard for the girls to get to sleep.'

'Girls, am I disturbing you? My bed creaks,' said Dusya loudly.

'No, you're not disturbing me,' answered Katya.

'Go ahead and creak if you have to,' Lyuba said and turned over under her blanket.

Nina was silent: she may have been asleep.

The doors to the rooms whined less and less often and, consequently, more noticeably.

5 Morning

'How much do I owe you?' asked Ivan Petrovich when he woke up the next morning.

'Thirty rubles,' said Dusya, without giving it a thought.

'Why thirty, specifically?' asked Ivan Petrovich. He was surprised, though fully prepared to pay.

'I owe this girl ten rubles, that one five, the one over there by the window eight, and the other seven I need to live on until payday,' Dusya replied quickly. 'Lyuba!' she called.

'Here I am,' said Lyuba, sticking her head out onto her pillow.

'Do I owe you ten rubles?'

'You do,' Lyuba confirmed and disappeared.

'Katya!' called Dusya.

'No, don't, why should you, I believe you,' said Ivan Petrovich. 'I just asked, that's all.'

'Katya,' said Dusya, not listening to Ivan Petrovich. 'Do I owe you five rubles?'

'Yes, you do, Dusya, that's right,' Katya replied, without turning her face towards Dusya.

'And I owe you eight, Nina?'

'Yes, eight,' replied Nina, lowering her legs from the bed, as though Ivan Petrovich were not there in the room.

'Do I need seven rubles myself to live on until payday?'

'Yes, you do,' said Nina. 'At least.'

'Seven rubles is just barely enough,' Lyuba corroborated.

Katya stood up in her nightgown on the bed and was already reaching out for her calendar.

'What's today?' she said. 'Let's have a look.'

And she turned over a few pages.

'Today there's an African proverb: "Don't push away the boat that helped you cross the river." '

She thought about the proverb.

'That's like our proverb, "Don't spit in the well" and so on.* They both say the very same thing! That means we and this African are neighbours in a way, right, Nina? We think almost the same way they do. Maybe they live like us too. It's just that they probably don't have wells or else they'd spit in them too.'

* In full the proverb is 'Don't spit in the well, you may have to drink the water.'

'I spent half my life in the river,' said Dusya, getting dressed. 'That's why all my proverbs are about fish.'

And it's true, her proverbs were about fish.

Lyuba laughed to herself about something and then explained: 'Here's another joke they like to play in the country: some yokel comes riding along on a horse and somebody shouts to him from the roadside, "Hey, you, rider, your horse has a collar on his neck!" He gets down, takes a look, and sure enough, the horse really has a collar on his neck. What a laugh.'

Everyone laughed and got up and got dressed, showing no concern that Ivan Petrovich was a man.

Ivan Petrovich got dressed bashfully.

'Maybe you want to go somewhere?' asked Dusya.

'No, no,' said Ivan Petrovich. 'It's quite all right.'

'Let him be patient for a bit,' remarked Nina. 'He can wash here. Lyuba, bring him some soap and water, let him get washed. He shouldn't go out now, he'll be noticed.'

Lyuba brought water in a jug and as she poured it out over a bowl for Ivan Petrovich he washed his face and hands.

'Now you'd better go,' said Dusya. 'And thanks a lot.'

'Wait a second, I'll peek out and see if the coast is clear,' Nina said, holding them back and going out into the corridor.

'OK, you can go,' she called. 'But hurry up! When you reach the second floor you can take your time, that's where the men live. Good-bye!'

In a moment, Ivan Petrovich found himself on the street.

6 Profoundly Symbolic

Barely waiting for the day's work to be over, Ivan Petrovich rushed back to the dorm.

He went as far as the bus stop with everyone else, but he did not stay there. Instead, he walked across the street and began waiting for a trolley going in the other direction. He stood facing all the people whom he was used to going home with and who – being used to him as well – were now eyeing him with suspicion across the tracks.

All the people who usually travelled with him were now travelling in the opposite direction.

7 The Hut

He stood near the entrance of the dormitory and paced back and forth a bit, waiting for Dusya to return from work.

'Hello,' said Dusya as she walked up to the dorm, as though they were seeing each other for the first time that day. 'What are you doing here? I've got enough money now until payday. I'm not going to need any more from now on, I'm not going to get into debt any more.'

'That's not it at all! I'd like to see you on different terms; that is, to meet you as if I were waiting for you and you came home,' Ivan Petrovich said very simply, something unusual for him, though his words were a little awkward.

'You mean you just wanted to meet me when I came home?' asked Dusya with understanding, after a brief deliberation.

'Yes,' Ivan Petrovich replied.

Dusya deliberated again.

'All right, but where will we go then?'

'The same place, to your room, in the dorm,' answered Ivan Petrovich.

'No, if things are like this it wouldn't be right to go to the dorm.'

'Why not? It was right yesterday, wasn't it?'

'Well, yesterday was different,' Dusya answered firmly. 'As it is now, we can't. Guests aren't supposed to be invited to the dormitory. We'd better go to the movies. Only, I'll pay for my own ticket.'

'Why should you pay? The man always pays for his date,' said Ivan Petrovich.

'I've got money now,' Dusya objected. 'I'll go, but I'll pay for myself.'

'Oh, all right,' Ivan Petrovich agreed. 'Have it your way.'

So off they went to a movie.

But it was too late for them to get in.

And once again Ivan Petrovich had a moment of resentful thought in this regard.

'The city, it keeps tempting you all the time,' thought Ivan Petrovich, instantly becoming incensed, 'and it always deceives you! Look at the smooth green grass in the park and on the square. But you're not allowed to lie around on it and loll about when you've an urge to. Look at the women, all dressed up, not hurrying anywhere, but you're not allowed to have them, at most only one as a last resort, and not always the best, and even then only with enormous difficulties, with close combat. Look at the movies, the sign lights up the street from one end to the other. But the tickets are all sold out by two o'clock!'

He had already raised his usual resentment to half pitch, but Dusya remarked placidly: 'Never mind. I wouldn't have gone to see that movie anyway.'

'How come?' Ivan Petrovich asked, and immediately calmed down – it wasn't clear why. 'Have you seen it?'

'No, I haven't seen it myself, but I've heard about it. It's all about fairness and I don't care for that sort of thing.'

'You mean you don't believe in fairness?' asked Ivan Petrovich.

'No, of course I do,' Dusya replied calmly. 'It's just that it's not the same for everybody. I don't like it when people urge me to be fair all the time but don't promise to be fair to me.'

'Who doesn't have the same kind of fairness as we do?' Ivan Petrovich asked with interest.

'Fairness is easier for people with nerve,' Dusya replied. 'They just grab it wherever they can.'

'And I suppose they really can,' thought Ivan Petrovich as the memory of his earlier behaviour flared up in him with shame and immediately disappeared.

'I know what,' Dusya said with determination. 'Forget the movie, let's find a park and go for a walk! I know a nice park.'

And off they went to the park.

They had to go by subway. Lottery tickets were enjoying a brisk sale in the station.

'A little money for a lot of happiness!' shouted the seller as he rotated the handle of this chance for happiness, emblazoned with a sign reading: 'Drawing tomorrow!'

Ivan Petrovich slowed his pace, let go of Dusya, and edged sideways a little, eyeing the revolving drum of tickets and imagining how he would go out of his mind with this cheap lottery happiness.

He had already reached into his pocket, was on the point of buying tickets for Dusya and himself, when suddenly it was 6 p.m. All at once the ticket-sellers finished their day's work. Snatching up chair and drum in one hand, they ran off to wherever they apparently kept them for the night. One of them, a fat man wearing a Persian lamb cap, ran through the crowd twice with a table under his arm, coming back for the galoshes he had left behind.

Ivan Petrovich was slightly miffed but he quickly noticed that Dusya had never once looked in the direction of the lottery and had not been enticed by that tempting happiness. He took a very long and interested look at her.

He and Dusya got on a train and soon arrived at the park.

By the entrance stood a cripple reeking of horses.

'Won't you be so kind?' he asked people with outstretched hand, inviting them to help provide him with refreshment. 'I wish you health and happiness!' He then offered his thanks and keeled forward slightly as a sign of courtesy.

A middle-aged man was leaving the park with his wife and kept speaking to her interestingly about the weather, continually calling her Irusya.

'Before work today,' Irusya spoke elatedly, 'I walked all the way to the factory!'

'And I went for a walk at lunch time today!'

'So then, how long were we out of doors today?'

On the bushes along the path bows of soft pink paper were tied at intervals, marking out a route of some sort. The bows were arranged in pairs: here were two together and then thirty paces further along two more. One of the pair was always high up, while the other, on the contrary, was tied to the lower branches. Evidently some couple had been past, and a picture was already emerging of that young man and woman and of what a good time they had had: each of them fashioning a bow on a bush, kissing, walking on a little way, then tying on another.

'On the whole, do you like me?' Ivan Petrovich suddenly asked. That's all he asked on this subject and then he fell silent.

'Yes,' Dusya replied readily. 'Except, you're very adult, but I like you anyway.'

'What do you mean by adult?' Ivan Petrovich asked.

'Oh, just adult, that's all. But that's not important. It may pass, if I make an effort,' Dusya said without explaining anything. And having said all she wanted on this subject, she took his hand.

Her hair was being tossed around by the wind, and as it

billowed, it revealed meandering glimpses of the delicate white crown underneath.

'People suppose I'm worse than others but I'm not,' said Dusya in a low voice. 'See, my face is nothing special, but the rest of me isn't bad and I've got a friendly nature.'

Rotating its head, a bird screamed out its chirping from a nearby tree.

'My hands are pretty bad,' Dusya continued. 'It's the kind of work I do, you know . . .'

For a long time she examined her hands, the round nail on the little finger, and the joint of the thumb merging into the edge of the palm, which she watched moving around inside there, in her palm, wrinkling the skin . . . and she began to marvel at it as though she were a child again.

From time to time Dusya would stop as if bitten on the leg by a gnat. With gentle, loving care, pausing at the calf, she would run a saliva-moistened finger along her leg to straighten her stocking.

From the opposite direction came a lone bulldog without its master. The bulldog walked peacefully, wagging its silk derrière like a lady and not deigning to look at passers-by.

The ribboned path led into a lane. The purpose of the pink bows immediately became clear: the lane was being used for races. Judging from the epaulettes worn by the band and the shirts folded up in the bushes, the races were being run by soldiers or other military men stationed in that area.

A lot of people had gathered near the finishing-line, spectators. They were all waiting for the runners.

Stretched across the lane was a banner reading: 'Onward to the Victory of Communism!'

Some kids with catapults were shooting at each other with obsolete ten-kopeck coins that had evaded exchange. The kopecks flew across the lane like tiny birds.

> 'We're buddies from Lugi
> And we dance the boogie-woogie,'

sang the buddies, tapping each other on the back and on the shoulder blades, but in no way dancing anything.

The musicians in the band got tired of sitting in their epaulettes with nothing to do; they scratched themselves beneath the bosom of their green uniforms and took up their instruments in concert.

The band began playing all by itself, without command. Kids stood around the musicians and gazed into their horns without blinking. Others put sticks in their mouths, pretending they were horns, and made faces. They puffed up their cheeks and squeezed the sides of the thin sticks, bowing with them in two directions, buckling their knees and barrelling out their bellies – but all in deadly earnest.

From somewhere out of the woods stepped the band-leader, who gave the band two notes with a sensitive finger and stepped away again.

One of the kids immediately made himself out to be the band-leader and then stopped, but continued blowing into his stick.

The bandleader walked around a little, played with the kids, sat on his heels, chased someone, and failing to overtake him, said, 'Quick, catch him!' He then returned to face the men in the band and conducted them a little more, although they were quite clearly not in the slightest need of it.

'Here they come!' said somebody nearby, and the band began to concentrate on a mazurka.

A tired athlete who was running slowly at full speed appeared in the lane.

A completely harmless drunk, his jacket clamped beneath his arm, stood amongst the spectators at the finishing-line. He would hang about for a bit, go stumbling out onto the path, and then back himself up again. It was he who spotted the runner coming down the lane.

'Here they come!' the drunk shouted loudly.

Just before the finishing-line the runner veered slightly from the path, while still moving, spat a bit of tasty sportive saliva into an urn so as not to sully the path and bespatter the whole park, and then put on a spurt and finished first.

The band struck up 'Fishing by the Riverside'.

The first runner was slowly followed by others. All the kids would run up alongside each one, down the edge of the lane and cross the finishing-line over and over again.

A motor cycle came to a grinding halt next to the finishing-line. Two generals, sporting trouser stripes and paunches, alighted from it.

Over to one side among the trees the winner, already dressed, was being cheerlessly tossed into the air. As he bobbed up and down, he remembered to hold onto his pocket, because a man is not meant to be turned upside down and if he is, all kinds of things start spilling from his pockets and often disappear irretrievably.

Some unhurried civilians ran by wearing spiked shoes and impeccable new uniforms and crossed the finishing-line so splendidly that one might have thought they were in the lead, rather than at the tail end.

Two men slowly rolled up the finishing-line and carried it off on their shoulders.

Then the banner was rolled up. It was carried forward, right after the finishing-line.

The two generals drove away in a car already containing a colonel.

'It's true,' observed Ivan Petrovich. 'Generals *are* fatter than colonels. I wonder why?'

The motor cycle was started up by a lean sergeant.

The band played on a little longer, then packed up.

The crowd dispersed.

Dusya and Ivan Petrovich walked on further into the park.

The park was gradually losing its lanes and becoming a small wood mowed clean by someone along the edges and between the bushes.

'You know,' said Ivan Petrovich sadly, 'I haven't walked through the grass without sandals in ten years. Is that silly?'

'Of course it's silly,' Dusya immediately agreed. 'Let your body live a little too, give it a stretch, bathe it in water. You can't just think of yourself; your body needs attention too.'

'Oh, I bathe it,' replied Ivan Petrovich. 'I bathe it, but not very often.'

Along the very edge of the park there was a pond. The water in the pond was level with its banks. Just as they were passing by a fisherman finally caught his little fish.

The boats of a nearby military sanatorium standing in formation on the smooth surface of the pond were beautifully painted in the colours of officers' uniforms.

Black fields ploughed under with winter crops opened up

in the distance beyond the pond. Flocks of seagulls scampered across the blackness of the ploughed earth.

'What are they doing there?' Ivan Petrovich genuinely wondered at the seagulls.

'They're looking for worms,' Dusya answered.

'What do you mean, "worms"? What do they need worms for? They live on fish, everybody knows that.'

'They need them to catch fish with,' Dusya said in all seriousness. 'I spent half my life in the river,' Dusya said once more. 'I know everything about fish.'

And it was true, she did know everything about fish.

Nearby, railway tracks ran through a ravine. Tandem locomotives were hauling a long train. A curly-haired signals operator, exposing her upper reaches as she bent over, was wiping the rails in her section with a dirty rag to prevent the stoppage of moving trains. In the sparse grass on the slope of the ravine stood a young man, slitting his eyes and rotating between his fingers a small leaf on a dry stem, while along a green path, the width of one not very wide foot, a cautious grey cat slowly made its way.

In the sky the sunset was beginning its daily game of variegation which we usually observe only if we are in the mood for looking into the distance.

Here he was on the street again, or rather, Ivan Petrovich sensed that he was on the street – he had such a keen conception of it. His mood was no longer on a basis sadness, but rather on a thoughtful, more solid one. Everything that wasn't home Ivan Petrovich called 'the street'.

'Looking at things close up, at a piece of paper, a book, or people you've met outside, reflected Ivan Petrovich very keenly, 'you can purposely unfocus your eye in such a way that you can't see what's in front of you, or else you can see it vaguely, in double silhouettes. It's impossible, however, to cloud your distance vision artificially; you can't distort it for yourself. Distant people, worldly phenomena – that is, those which are around us, far off – will appear to us just the way we see them. All you can do is turn away and not look at them at all.'

Ivan Petrovich turned away, began to look at Dusya, and led her off into the distance.

On the other side of the tracks the park continued again. It became even wilder and more dense. They came upon white-kneed birches; young populars with shaggy trunks; the round, oily leaves of bushes growing green as soon as they emerged from the ground; small glades flecked with raspberry blossoms – amid yellow, forgotten, stagnant grass.

They stepped out into this raspberry colour and saw a hut in the middle of the glade. Put together out of all kinds of withered branches, the hut stood firmly on the flesh of the earth. It had been abandoned by people. No one had lived in it for a long time, but inside a matting of grass was still intact. Two wattled walls propped each other up, preventing the hut from collapsing in on itself.

'How on earth is a hut constructed?' ran through Ivan Petrovich's mind. 'They take two walls and forcibly bend each wall towards the one opposite it. The walls fall, but since they run into each other, come up against each other, they are held in place and won't ever fall any further, continuing to stand obliquely, supported by one another. And within this shaky space it is perfectly possible to live, even for a very great person – which once was indeed the case in recent times.'

He felt an urge to get inside the hut. He recalled one of his main childhood impressions, one of his few trips to the country. He was sitting in a hayloft all alone, and it was raining. He had covered himself with his grandmother's yellow sheepskin coat and was looking out of a small window at the rain. The hayloft leaked; through a crack in the ceiling large drops kept trickling down one by one. The drops struck resonantly against the tanned hide and increased Ivan Petrovich's – then it was simply Vanya's – feeling of pleasure from the sturdy protection.

'It's raining, but the rain can't do anything to me!' was all he kept thinking.

The girl next door came. Her name was Tanya or, as everyone called her, Tanyusha, and she was the same age as he was, about thirteen or perhaps a little more. Tanyusha took a quarter of his coat, covered her shoulders and the back of her head, and also began looking out of the window. The hayloft was common to the entire house, half of which was his grandmother's, while Tanya's father lived in the other half.

Vanya liked her, as, incidentally, he liked many others with whom he had gone to school and grown up. But after he had moved away to the city, it was she alone whom he would recall in a special way, and the devil only knows how far he went with her in his imagination.

He imagined of course that it would be summer, and not in the city. He and Tanyusha would get undressed in some room, undressed not like at the beach, but meaningfully, and they would stay naked. Outdoors there would have to be a downpour of rain that wouldn't frighten them even though it would loudly batter against everything conceivable. He would touch her unclothed slender side, and she would touch his shoulder, and then his ribs. They would graze each other so lightly and shiver from the cold fingers against the skin. That was all he imagined then; but even then what seemed most important to him, most decisive, was what he would feel when it happened: how they would arrive at such a bold decision, what words they would speak beforehand which might make them feel ashamed – not of each other but of themselves, inwardly, because of the awkwardness and the hurried drive onward, to get down to business, as it were; words which could make them enemies and through that very enmity achieve what they both envisaged; and, finally, words which could leave them a slight embarrassment for their greater joy, and together with that embarrassment would permit them to trust each other so much, and so overcome the distrust and fear of the other's reaction that the allure of another person, perceived through revealed outlines and the softness of the body, the touch of cold fingers, the shivering, and through the retarded flow of time, would create for them a day of such happiness as no two people had ever achieved.

But it never happened like this with Tanyusha. Nor did it ever happen like this with anyone else, though in general quite a lot had happened to him.

And right now he really felt like going into the hut, only he did not know how Dusya would react to this.

And as if she had perceived what he had just been thinking, Dusya stooped down and got into the hut. Ivan Petrovich hurriedly climbed in too as far as he could. His feet extended outside. Dusya was hanging over him slightly. He cupped his

hand tentatively around her neck, gently drawing her large,
naturally raspberry-red mouth towards him. Her strong neck
did not yield at once, and Ivan Petrovich had already prepared
himself for his usual vexation. But then Dusya herself planted
his mouth against her lips and kissed him long and hard. Then
she broke into a laugh and wiped her mouth with the back of
her hand.

Ivan Petrovich also burst out laughing at himself, at this lack
of confidence which he had felt but which had now completely
disappeared. Suddenly he was overcome with tenderness
for Dusya because of her understanding; the tender feeling
gushed through him from his ears down to his heels and began
moving about, tingling, and looking for a way out. He felt
that his greatest desire was to let his head drop onto Dusya's
knees. And he granted himself this desire and let his head
drop onto her sharply-angled knees, something he would never
have allowed himself before. He twisted his head around across
those knees, clasped his hands around them backwards over his
shoulders, and began looking upwards at Dusya's face, her
round chin, her lips obliquely receding into her mouth, her hair
hanging down over one eye. He reached out and moved it away
from the eye. He was in want of nothing else, he felt. From
below rose a smell of rotting grass. Some twigs worked themselves loose and were falling onto his face. Thin, dry wisps of bark
streamed in the air from the movements that swayed the hut.

Something nearly landed in his eyes, but his eyes managed to
shield themselves; something had been drawn up into his nose
and his nose started to tickle. Light tears welled up in his eyes
without spilling. His chest heaved as he took an excessive,
monstrous breath, and Ivan Petrovich loudly and happily
sneezed at the entire glade, first once and then again. He
stopped, his eyes slitted, and waited for a third time, but the
third time would not come.

Dusya laughed.

'You're just like me. You're also one sneeze short of happiness,' she said.

Ivan Petrovich waited, with his cheeks wrinkled and his lips
puckered up towards his nose, thinking the sneeze would never
come, and in fact it never did. Aggrieved, he gradually relaxed
his face again until it was smooth.

'Yes,' he answered Dusya in astonishment. 'I guess so.'

And now he and Dusya had one of those real conversations between two people, when each one talks about himself and the other just happens to find it interesting.

Later this conversation continued for the rest of their lives.

'Well, I . . .' Dusya would say. 'With me . . .'

'No, but I . . .' Ivan Petrovich would say.

'Now, I, for example,' Dusya would say again.

'Yes, yes!' Ivan Petrovich would agree. 'Me, too!'

Someone was roaming about in the bushes, making muffled noises.

'We ought to clear out of here,' Ivan Petrovich thought, suddenly feeling uneasy.

He hesitated before saying so to Dusya, but Dusya herself, on her own, arrived at the same thought at that very moment and hurriedly prepared to leave the park.

They had no wish now for the superfluous eyes of others.

They crawled out of the hut and straightened themselves up a bit. They crossed the glade, and then the railway track with its signals. They were already nearing the front half of the park.

On the path in the distance appeared the same man, holding the leaf stem. He approached them very rapidly, like an express train.

'Well, had yourselves a nice walk?' he asked, slitting his eyes at them. He added a blunt, foul remark in the form of a question – and then quickly strode off past them.

The remark itself did not arouse in Ivan Petrovich the anger that it would have in an affected, inveterate old maid who has never heard such things or read them on fences. 'There aren't any people like that around,' he sometimes thought. 'Or are there?' But just like that, said right to your face, and in front of Dusya, it was offensive, and made him want to dash after that scoundrel, who had in any case already vanished without a trace down the path, and then dash back to Dusya, to prevent her from feeling as if something had happened, and use different words to blot out of her hearing the remark made by the man with the slitted eyes.

But just then Dusya burst out laughing and said good-naturedly: 'What a pig! He talks with pictures!'

Ivan Petrovich did not understand at first.

'We had one like that in our village too, Slovanty Romanych,' said Dusya. 'He sang. There's a lot of that in the country. In our village it's not considered anything special if you can sing. But he would have been admired for his voice in the city. I've never heard a voice as loud as his. True, he didn't carry the tune very well but his voice was loud. Slovanty Romanych would climb up on a roof or a haystack and sing out to the whole village. His songs were all like that, with pictures, strong pictures! He'd sing and we'd laugh. What a nerve!' she added, recalling him vividly.

With pictures, Ivan Petrovich realised, meant with obscenities. And now he felt a sense of ease with Dusya. They had a good laugh and completely forgot about the man with the slitted eyes.

On the edge of the woods, in a completely desolate spot, for some reason there was suddenly a cart standing there, and from it a lady wearing a white smock, not so much white but dazzling amidst the dark green forest of bushes and trees, was selling fried rusty brown *pirozhki*.

'These are good *pirozhki*,' the vendor confided. 'Have some yourselves and tell others about 'em. You, young lady, tell everybody they can get *pirozhki* here!'

'All right,' Dusya agreed. 'I will.'

There wasn't anybody to tell, even if one made a real effort.

'Let's tell the guy with the pictures!' Ivan Petrovich suggested, and laughed heartily.

Dusya, also, burst out laughing over this.

They laughed for a long time, bending at the knees and leaning against each other in laughter, and again rollicking backwards with laughter.

'Him, the one with the squint!' said Dusya through her laughter.

'With the pictures!' Ivan Petrovich guffawed.

'And the leaf! . . .'

'We'll tell him all right!'

A watermelon carefully wrapped in newspaper, with a lot of folds, corners, and tucks, was carried by close to the ground in a long string bag. It looked as if someone wanted to conceal the fact that there was a watermelon inside the newspaper, as if it could ever be concealed.

'Look,' Ivan Petrovich whispered, holding back his previous laughter. 'You know what that is?'

'What?' asked Dusya weakly, expecting a new round of laughter.

'It's a watermelon!' he shouted to the world, and once again became convulsed.

'Ah-ha-ha!' Dusya laughed, exhausting all her air until she began to wheeze. 'Well, I'll be ...! A watermelon! I didn't know that!'

'Anyone, just anyone can tell it's a watermelon!' Ivan Petrovich dissolved in laughter, as if he weren't an adult. Dusya, too, kept laughing so hard that at times she even felt a bit frightened.

They had a good laugh and then gradually began to calm down. They squeezed the tears from their eyes with their fingers, flung them onto the path, and fell silent. Only from time to time did they emit brief gurgles of residual laughter, but now they tried not to encourage each other.

'Hey, what about those *pirozhki*, did we forget?' reminded Dusya.

They settled down and began eating *pirozhki*.

'Hey, it's empty, this *pirozhok*,' said Ivan Petrovich after taking a bite.

'No,' Dusya replied earnestly. 'These *pirozhki* have jam in them. I know.'

He took another bite.

'No, it's empty.'

'That's the kind of *pirozhki* they are,' Dusya explained. 'Eat them and think: Be still, my heart, soon it will be sweet!'

And soon it really did become sweet.

8 *Average Prices*

A month later Dusya moved in with Ivan Petrovich.

They did not go down to the Clerk's Office to make it official. He couldn't just up and go to the powers-that-be and ask for permission, which, he believed, was what it really amounted to. All the same, he had to get used to the idea.

After all, if everything were normal, as it should be, Ivan

Petrovich reasoned at first, no one would ask a married man: Are you a good man?

'Here's my wife, this woman here finds it possible to love me all the time, without interruption' – that's how he would answer them – when married, that is. And that would be quite sufficient.

'Hah-hah!' people would say in reply. 'Hah-hah-hah! Anyone can be loved ... for a while! Then it's over ... so what? The woman loves you, you think! But she herself, the woman, what sort of person is she? Does she really love you? Maybe it's just something she simply needs? Who knows anything about her anyway?'

'And she, she's the kind of person I'm not in the least bit timid about loving in front of everybody,' – that's the way to answer them, very firmly.

'So you say you love each other! Hah-hah! It's like two cripples bent over and leaning on each other ... and holding each other up. Big deal! No, that doesn't prove a thing. That's not it at all.'

'And they're right, on the whole,' Ivan Petrovich agreed. 'All the scoundrels that are around are married too – or aren't they?'

Because of this Ivan Petrovich delayed going to that office for a long while, but later he became somewhat reconciled to the idea and did go.

It cannot be said that Ivan Petrovich had entered a period of complete tranquillity with Dusya.

True, he no longer got worked up when he saw people on the street. The pleasure he gained through his eyes was reduced and confined to Dusya, and no longer disturbed him so painfully. Saturated with the view of one person very close to them they now took in objects more often.

Sometimes, while he was making breakfast for himself before going to work, Ivan Petrovich would become engrossed in looking into the frying-pan and observing the egg-shell crack against its cast-iron side; the time it took to pour it out of each half was endless. He watched the *pelmeni* cook in boiling water – if you didn't watch out they would lose almost all their clothing. He would look at the apple that Dusya liked to eat in the morning and watch her gnaw all round it and up from the bottom.

Ivan Petrovich liked to look at all this in the mirror, not at himself but at the room. He liked the mirror and its life in reverse, from right to left, as it were, and its pure space among the objects. Even the dirt and disorder were reflected in the mirror as though captured in their continuing state, in other words, like a picture that has its own beauty and interest.

But at times dark, elemental forces of mutual irritation came down upon Ivan Petrovich and Dusya.

One Saturday Ivan Petrovich left the factory a little late, having been slightly detained.

The main entrance had already quietened down and was empty of people. The guard stood trustfully to one side, entertaining no suspicions about people who were so serious and responsible that they didn't go home on time even on a Saturday.

After seeing to the Saturday exodus through the gates the head of security, happy and relaxed, himself set out for his familial, ordinary, unguarded home.

After seeing the factory off to rest, the personnel manager made his way out. Catching up with his staff, who were lagging a bit, he overtook them effortlessly because he was less tired, after all, from his telephone calls and difficult forms. The manager hurried as fast as he could to assert himself at home, in his masculine fishing and hunting life.

His staff also rushed off to this same life.

Ivan Petrovich dropped in at a store to buy all sorts of food to please Dusya. He now always wanted to bring Dusya everything she liked.

There were a lot of people in the store. The entire factory had gone over to the stores opposite, to buy food on the way and then eat their fill at home. And other factories and institutes had gone to other stores.

Ivan Petrovich stood patiently. Altogether he stood for about an hour. He bought butter, sugar, a bottle of cream, tomatoes, a brown loaf and a small white. He had already bought more than he could carry. Ivan Petrovich did not have a string bag.

Just then he saw some watermelons for sale. 'I'll buy her a watermelon,' thought Ivan Petrovich, delighting in himself. 'Never mind, I'll carry it home somehow, I'm sure I can.'

The purchase of a watermelon is a matter so obscure, so dark, concealed within itself beneath the green rind, that the queue was stirring about in muffled commotion, demanding the impossible from the watermelons. Someone wanted to squeeze one until it cracked; he was not allowed to squeeze one until it cracked. Someone asked to pick one out, but he was refused. Someone tried to roll one out from the side – but he just couldn't manage to roll it out.

'Next!' the saleslady would shout. 'What do you want?'

'A watermelon!' the next in line would reply, as though asking for something different, even though all they sold here was watermelons.

The saleslady would bend down, plunge into the pen, and drag to the surface whatever she fished out from down there in the dense mass. After slinging it from one palm to the other next to her ear and for appearance sake kneading it and producing an imaginary cracking sound, she would weigh it approximately and a moment later she would toss the watermelon onto the counter.

The customer would open his purse, then close it; he'd vacillate, unhappy with the speed of the operation, and be afraid. The queue was unhappy with the customer, and everyone was unhappy with the saleslady, and together they expressed the people's smouldering discontent with the watermelons.

Ivan Petrovich hardly said a word, except maybe to ask for the biggest, the very best, and the saleslady yelled at him, the queue yelled at him, Ivan Petrovich yelled at the saleslady and at the queue and became sorely flustered.

As he walked away with a small watermelon under his arm, holding the rest of the food against his chest, Ivan Petrovich, just because he was upset, suddenly felt weak, staggered, let go of the bread and sugar, and dropped the bottle of cream and the tomatoes. The watermelon somehow stayed under his arm.

Ivan Petrovich got down on his haunches, took the watermelon in both hands, and sat there for a long time. The saleslady shouted something in his direction, something that prevailed against all dim-witted and insolent customers.

Some of the sugar spilled and the bottle broke. The cream poured onto the tomatoes and the white bread. Someone took the hapless watermelon from Ivan Petrovich and held it for him. Ivan Petrovich gathered up everything he could, took the watermelon without a thank you, and left the store with a feeling of total and bitter resentment.

He thought of Dusya and the purchases he had made on her behalf and felt like taking out his resentment on her. He wanted her to feel responsible.

He held his vexation in his mouth all the way home, and kept shutting his lips tightly for fear of losing it all. He turned, climbed the stairs, pressed the bell with his forehead, and, unable to hold it in any longer, shouted through the door:

'I'm never going to the store again!'

Dusya jumped up quickly to open the door. He piled everything he was carrying onto the table and then ranted bitterly about everything – about shopping, about people who apparently have to buy everything all at once, and about the fact that she should give him a string bag.

Dusya began crying and went off to the sofa.

Ivan Petrovich, too, went over to the sofa and lay down with his back turned to Dusya, nursing his resentment against her for not holding herself to blame and for not soothing him in his distress, as she could so easily have done.

After lying there a little while, he jumped up and went into the kitchen to cut open the watermelon. The watermelon was pink and clearly not ripe. This upset Ivan Petrovich completely; he went back and fell straight away onto the sofa.

They lay like that on the same wide sofa, turned away from each other, each facing his own irritation.

After lying in silence for about half an hour, Ivan Petrovich came round a little and suddenly understood about Dusya. He understood that she would like to cuddle up against him as if she were frail, as if she were a lot smaller and didn't want to know about him, that he was in need of something, that he too could turn out to be frail. She wanted him to shelter her like something solid, while he himself wanted to cuddle up against someone (her), he himself wanted to have someone shield him (not all the time, however; only when it was badly needed), because he was not at all the subduer of nature, the Jack London type, whom she had hoped to find in him.

'But here I'm making a mistake, of course,' reflected Ivan Petrovich, growing calmer and wiser. 'Support like that should go in levels: I cuddle up against someone who's higher, and she cuddles up against me, because one can't be both strong and weak simultaneously in relation to the very same thing. A ceiling can't be the floor for this room, but for the next room right above – it's very simple. Before, all of this was much easier; a man had a mother for this: the wife took comfort in him and he took comfort in his mother. And she would be supported and sheltered by the father. And because he had lived a very long time, the father was already accustomed to being his own protective cover – or else he sought consolation in some sort of business, as long as he could.

'Now, most of our fathers were killed at the front, or scattered, or else they couldn't endure their specially trained state wives and left or died, tired to death of living. And our mothers remain alone now, without protection, and although they'd like to they are no longer able to pass down to us – their sons – their protection, their support, which adults, not children need, and we huddle up against our wives for that: "Stay here and lean on my shoulder, for an instant the two of us together are in the middle of life," wrote the poet.'

Half an hour was spent with this thought. Then Ivan Petrovich got tired and fell asleep.

Suddenly, in his sleep, life became better for Ivan Petrovich. He awoke to have an outside look at what had happened. Dusya lay there embracing him with her sleepy elbow, as if there were no resentment between them. She was embracing him with her sleep. She had let one leg fall to the side and had rested her knee against Ivan Petrovich.

Ivan Petrovich felt unusually peaceful. In this common, united, and mutual sleep with a woman all the hurts and all the worries about the direction of life had vanished somewhere.

'How come I never read about this kind of thing in books?' Ivan Petrovich thought regretfully. 'Maybe I would have begun living differently. Of course, I did come across something in some old classics. Only, I didn't believe it for a minute then. It's not that I didn't believe it – why not? I simply didn't realise that they were talking about me. They were all books about the hard life of people who *don't have to go to work*.

'Why, that's it, why, of course,' he suddenly understood and frowned briefly. 'This sort of thing must not be written about in art, not in our art, so that our enemies never find out how an ordinary Soviet man sleeps with a woman. Well, never mind, we'll get along somehow without necessary books like that.'

By the clock it was about three in the morning. In spite of this, the light was ablaze in the room. A fly flew about, bumping into the walls. It made a circle round the lamp and continued bumping. The fly, too, was suffering because of them and not sleeping, thinking it was merely evening and that it was supposed to be this way.

Ivan Petrovich turned off the light and intended to fall asleep, but a new worry was developing in him. He couldn't forgive himself for not being able to think of such a mutual life a lot sooner.

'This is how life is divided,' ran through Ivan Petrovich's mind. 'It takes us a long time to establish our concepts of happiness and truth, then in accordance with those concepts we begin to undertake things. But even before the concepts are fully established we have to do something anyway, on faith, because a man can't just sit back idly, because of the circumstances, and after all, it often seems as if this is it – truth; here it is – happiness. Certain stages in the process – ledges – we are in a great hurry to take as the summit; because, ultimately, for many people the first period drags on for a long time, sometimes virtually for ever – in that case what should be done, not begin at all?

'And it often turns out that by the time we know everything – how to act, how we are to live in accordance with freedom and truth, with happiness – we have already begun to live differently, we've begun something else, not natural to us, as it were. We've begun relationships not with the kind of people we wanted to – and it's impossible to do anything about it, just as impossible as going out for a stroll around French Guiana or moving to Chicago and starting a new life there under a new name.' (Ivan Petrovich had read these words in some book and they'd stuck in his mind ever since.)

Oh, if a man knew that all his words and acts immediately become a part of his composite fate, if it were possible to make him feel this and keep it with him and always remember it with every word – then he would never do anything that was not beneficial to his own fate or anything he feared might be of harm to it; then everyone would stand to benefit. Thoughtless, improvident words and actions would sharply decrease, and this would start having a remarkable influence on our lives, our work, and the social order.

That's why so many different books are preoccupied with showing fate – it's to show by example, to demonstrate, to allow us to feel how our actions, our conversations are immediately recorded in some book of life from which later there is no escape.

'But I,' thought Ivan Petrovich, poking his head out from under the blanket onto the pillow, 'I hadn't begun anything before I established myself. I didn't start to live differently until I understood.'

He conscientiously began to convince himself that this must be so, by recalling that crucial time when he had changed his course of study. Having succeeded in convincing himself, he tried to fall asleep again, but happiness no longer allowed him to sleep.

'How does personal happiness come about?' was yet another thought that struck Ivan Petrovich. 'At the price of renouncing the liberty of the unhampered life, which ultimately leads to loneliness (and I have renounced it). At the price of increased concern for family, salary, a home. At the price of submission to one's superiors. (I managed to do this too – after all, I did go down to the Clerk's Office, didn't I?) At the price of suppressing in one's self unnecessary cravings for the unexpected, at the price of cultivating in one's self a quiet, modest life. These are the average prices of our personal, family happiness. There are many who can never ever achieve it. Or, maybe, they don't want it?'

Ivan Petrovich sat up on his elbow, made out Dusya, who was sleeping quietly in the darkness, sleeping together with him in harmony in the same, shared sleep, and in the darkness he shook his head to himself:

'No, they just can't!'

And with the awareness of what he had managed to achieve, what he had managed to find and what he had managed to suppress, Ivan Petrovich fell asleep without any difficulty.

9 The Need to Be . . .

'You may go down to the mine face!' he'd sing in the morning as he headed for work, though he wasn't going down to the mine face.

'You may cut your way into the rock!' sang Ivan Petrovich, quickening his steps, though he didn't cut his way into the rock, either; but that's not important.

Ivan Petrovich liked to go to work.

Of course, it's no fun getting up in the morning. It's so early. And, of course, when you ride on the bus you get pushed. And the weather's nice in the summer; in the summer you want to be out in the sun.

'But all the same, honestly, I like work,' Ivan Petrovich admitted to himself. He liked to calculate the overall gain because he was an economist, and this was his business.

Here they were, walking past the fountain at the factory. Out of the ground, out of a grill, steam came shooting up. The figure of a female athlete was set in the fountain – a nice, robust lass holding an oar. The workers were fond of this figure and always discussed it when they passed by.

'For some reason the old girl is drizzling onto the walk today. She doesn't like the weather, it's windy, so she's spraying passers-by.'

'It was thirty years ago that she got undressed and she's been standing there undressed ever since.'

'My, she must be cold! Especially in winter.'

Every year she was given a fresh coat of silver paint, and every year the paint made her stouter and stouter. Her broken-off fingers had been replaced with grafts of cement which were growing right into the shaft of the oar.

'Underneath she's thin,' said Galya Morina from shop No. 1. 'It's true, she's thin, I remember. She's got a nice figure even.'

A newspaper once said about the factory: 'In the grounds there is a place to relax at lunchtime. Flowers grow everywhere and cool streams gush from fountains.' Ivan Petrovich was amused by this. That's the way those newspaper people are: they take a stroll around the factory, see the fountain and make a note of it, and then compose something about cool streams. Ivan Petrovich began to feel a slight disrespect for newspaper people.

This funny, homely fountain, a triumph of bad taste, had not at all been intended for cool streams at lunch. Ivan Petrovich knew what the fountain was here for; he figured out how much advantage it brought the factory. The water gushing in the fountain was recirculated and went into the shops to cool the generators. This recirculated water, from a single intake, made efficient use of the available water-supply.

Ivan Petrovich was very fond of that homely fountain.

Your job, if you like it and are competent at it, is the only place on earth (thought Ivan Petrovich) where you're not afraid of anybody, where you always know exactly what to do and how to do it at any given moment, where you are always sure you are right and are necessary. And this is something every person has to know.

Of course, sometimes even at work somebody may offend you – it's not always a bed of roses. Ivan Petrovich was recently offended by his boss. 'But that's all right, let them offend me now and then, I'm strong,' Ivan Petrovich conceded. 'After all, he didn't do it on purpose, I'm not mad at him. He was just doing his job, it wasn't anything personal.'

Whenever he left the factory, he wasn't without support for long. When the shift was over, he'd go straight to meet Dusya.

Their frequent need to be together continued to grow stronger and broader, although it did not continue to increase their pleasure. By now they were already leaning on each other, and there was no end to this in sight because for both of them it replaced a freedom from each other which they did not need. This already constituted dependence because their concepts, their notions of truth and happiness, kept adjusting to each other with a better and better fit, and a world had already begun to take shape 'in the midst of life'; and in that world they loved each other because of the unlimited possibility for understanding; yet this kind of dependence also contained a touch of resentment – perhaps not so slight – which led to ephemeral, trivial arguments that became more and more frequent and, at the same time, increasingly mild – which was also a cause for resentment!

Ivan Petrovich would sometimes look at Dusya and think: 'They wanted to offend you and, of course, readily would

have. They wanted to offend me, too, and might have succeeded. But we grasped hold of each other in time and out-
witted them! And now they can't do anything to us as long as
we just keep it within, between ourselves, and don't give in to
temperament, mood or other minor everyday enemies.'

Ivan Petrovich now never tried to explain himself who 'they'
were, and how they might have offended the two of them;
it never even crossed his mind, but he felt it strongly.

'Their life might have been hell, but she didn't allow it,'
said the neighbours, whose observations are cursory but who
notice everything.

And therefore he and Dusya were already living heart to
heart – and this was noticeable even from outward appearances,
from the way they walked along the street: shoulder to shoulder,
step for step, hand in hand, head to head.

He pretended a little to be very sincere and gentle – yet
while he pretended, he really was – is that so bad?

His flimsy jacket, blown every which way by the wind,
revealed his shirt and his short tie fluttering to the side, over
his shoulders and beyond.

The sleeve of his jacket got between their palms, untwining
their fingers, and vexed them both . . .

1964

Biographical Notes

JOSEPH BRODSKY Born in Russia in 1940. Persecuted in his homeland for his literary activity, he was rarely published there and only then primarily as a translator of Polish and English poetry. In June, 1972, he was forced to leave the Soviet Union. Since then he has been living in the United States and is currently Poet-in-Residence and Professor of Russian at the University of Michigan. A volume of his poetry, *Selected Poems*, was published in English in 1973.

MILOVAN DJILAS Born in 1911 in Polya, Montenegro, the son of a police officer, he went to Belgrade to study law in 1929. Imprisoned for being a Communist, 1933–37. Member of the Central Committee and the Politbureau of the Communist Party of Yugoslavia, 1937. He was a close collaborator with Tito during the partisan struggles, and in 1945 was appointed Minister Without Portfolio. In 1953, Djilas stood up in favour of the democratisation of the Party in Yugoslavia. In 1954 he was expelled from the Politbureau and relieved of all official positions and duties. Two months later, he resigned from the Party. Arrested in 1956 for criticising Yugoslavia's position with regard to the Hungarian uprising, he was condemned to three years in prison. He was sentenced to an additional seven years in the penitentiary for his book, *The Price of Freedom*, and resentenced in 1962 for publishing *Conversations With Stalin*. In prison he wrote a novel with the working title 'Worlds and Bridges' (translated into German in 1972), and a volume of short stories. He was pardoned in 1966, but forbidden to publish. In 1968, *The Execution* was published, and in 1969, *The Unperfect Society* appeared in the West. *The New Class*, forbidden in Yugoslavia, appeared in the West in 1957. Milovan Djilas lives in Belgrade, Yugoslavia.

ALEXANDER ARKADEVICH GALICH Born 19 October, 1919. He began writing as a very young man. After graduating from the Stanislavsky Studio, Galich served in the front line during the war. In 1945 he began working as a dramatist. Ten of Galich's plays have been staged in the USSR, among them *The Taimyr is Calling You*,

Weekdays and Weekends, and *Campaign March*. His best dramatic works, however, have been denied public performance. Galich has also worked a good deal for the cinema; he was involved in making *Faithful Friends*, *The State Criminal*, *To the Seven Winds* and many other films.

In the early 1960s Galich became widely known as a writer and singer. Home-made tape recordings of his songs spread throughout the country. The topical content of his work and its sharply satirical political orientation led to persecution by the authorities. On 29 December, 1971, Galich was expelled from the Union of Writers, the Union of Cinematographers and the Literary Fund (the welfare organisation of Soviet writers). Hounded on all sides, he was forced to leave the Soviet Union. He went abroad in June 1974 and now lives in Norway.

He has published four books in the West in Russian: *Poem of Russia*, *Songs*, *Generation of the Accursed*, and *The Dress Rehearsal*.

IGOR NAUMOVICH GOLOMSHTOK Born in 1929. An art historian, he graduated in history of art at Moscow University. He worked as a senior researcher at the Pushkin State Museum of Representative Art in Moscow. He also lectured at Moscow University and worked in the All-Union Scientific and Research Institute of Technical Aesthetics. He was a member of the Union of Soviet Artists. He is the author of a number of books and monographs on the history and theory of western European art. Since 1972 he has been living in Great Britain, lecturing at the universities of St Andrews and Oxford.

VLADIMIR RAFAILOVICH MARAMZIN Born on 5 August, 1934, in a village near Leningrad. In 1957 he graduated from the Leningrad Electrotechnical Institute and worked for eight years as an engineer. He is the author of several children's books which have appeared in Soviet publications, and has written scripts and scenarios for films, TV, and radio. For many years he also wrote unusually inventive prose, often satirical, which could not be published in the USSR. In April, 1974, his apartment was searched and all his manuscripts were confiscated, as well as his typewriter. In July, 1974, he was arrested and charged with collecting the 'works of an anti-Soviet person', Joseph Brodsky. He was held in prison until February, 1975, when he was tried on charges of writing slanderous material against the USSR and distributing anti-Soviet literature. He was given a suspended sentence of five years with three years' probation. In the summer of 1975 he was allowed to leave the USSR and now lives in Paris.

ALEXANDER MOYSEYEVICH PIATIGORSKY Born in 1929 in

Moscow. Russian buddhologist and student of Eastern philosophy. He graduated from Moscow University and took his doctorate in Indian philology. He became a researcher at the Institute for the Peoples of Asia and Africa, then lectured at Moscow University. From the early 1960s he worked together with Lotman, Ivanov and Toporov to create a new school of semiotics. He is the author of a number of monographs and articles about philosophy, Hinduism and Buddhism, which have been translated into many European languages. Since 1974 he has lived in England.

ANDREI DMITRIEVICH SAKHAROV Born in 1921 in Moscow. In 1938 he entered Moscow University, where he graduated in physics in 1942. For the rest of the war he worked in a munitions factory, then for three years did post-graduate studies under the famous physicist Igor Tamm. He then joined a special research group developing nuclear weapons for the Soviet armed forces. Simultaneously, with Tamm, he was conducting research into controlled thermo-nuclear reactions and formed an idea of magnetic thermo-isolation of high-temperature plasma. This work continued until 1968, during which time he was awarded the Stalin prize, the Hero of Socialist Labour Medal and elected a full member of the Soviet Academy of Sciences. In 1961 he entered into discussion with Nikita Khrushchev about the peaceful use of nuclear energy. His first public statement was in 1966, when, with others, he signed an appeal asking the new Soviet leadership not to rehabilitate Stalin. In 1968 he made his views on disarmament and peaceful co-existence more widely known, as a result of which he was dismissed from all his posts in August of that year. He then began his social work, dealing with the problems of Soviet citizens imprisoned or persecuted for political reasons, his only formal post being that of a researcher at the Lebedev Institute of Physics. His works *Progress, Coexistence and Intellectual Freedom*, *Sakharov Speaks* and *My Country and the World* have been published in Britain. In 1975 he was awarded the Nobel Peace Prize.

ANDREI DONATOVICH SINYAVSKY Born in 1925 in Moscow. Russian writer and literary critic. He graduated from Moscow University and continued post-graduate work in philology at the Institute of World Literature. He was one of the leading critics on the literary journal *Novy Mir* and has written about twentieth-century Russian poetry. In 1955 he began to have his work published abroad under the name Abram Terz, for example *Lyubimov*, *Fantastic Stories* and the article *What is Socialist Realism?* For this he was expelled from the Union of Writers in 1965, arrested and sentenced. He spent six years in strict régime camps in Mordovia, working as a porter and loader. In 1973 he left Russia to live in France. His book *A Voice from the Chorus* appeared in Russian soon after he moved abroad, in English early in 1976. At present he is a professor at the Sorbonne University in Paris.

ALEXANDER ISAYEVICH SOLZHENITSYN Born in 1918, graduated in mathematics at Rostov University. Served as a Captain of Artillery in the Second World War before being arrested in 1945, after which he spent eight years in labour camps. After his release he lived some years in exile in Central Asia before being rehabilitated. His novel *One Day in the Life of Ivan Denisovich* was published in 1962 and was followed by several shorter stories in the Moscow journal *Novy Mir*. His two novels *Cancer Ward* and *The First Circle* were first published in the West in 1968. In 1970 he was awarded the Nobel Prize for Literature. His novel *August 1914*, the first of a series on the years leading up to the Russian Revolution, appeared in 1971. In February 1974, he was forcibly expelled from the Soviet Union. The first volume of *Gulag Archipelago*, a series of books about Stalin's labour camps, appeared shortly afterwards. He now lives with his family in Zurich.

CARL-GUSTAV STRÖHM Born in Estonia in 1930. He studied East European History at the University of Tübingen, Germany, and obtained his doctorate with a dissertation on Lenin's military politics in the Russian civil war. In 1966, he was appointed Director of the Southeastern-Europe Programme of Deutsche Welle Radio; in 1972, political correspondent of the Munich paper, *Die Welt*. Author of *Between Mao and Khrushchev* and *From the Tsar's Empire to the Soviet Power*.

ANTHONY SAMPSON

THE SEVEN SISTERS

ESSO, GULF, TEXACO, MOBIL, CHEVRON, BP and SHELL
– seven huge companies which have dominated the world of oil – and all our lives – since Rockefeller's first gigantic oil monopoly. The energy crisis in the West caused a shift of power towards the Arab and Iranian producers : but into whose hands will control of oil fall, or should it fall, in the future ?

'A book that will help us understand the most profound economic changes of our time'
New York Times Book Review

CORONET BOOKS

VICTOR MARCHETTI & JOHN D MARKS

THE CIA AND THE CULT OF INTELLIGENCE

WHAT IS THE CIA REALLY UP TO? WHAT GOES ON BEHIND THE IMPENETRABLE SCREEN OF SECURITY?

When Victor Marchetti, for nine years a senior CIA official, set out to answer these pressing and frequent questions, he at once became the first American writer to be subjected to government censorship before his book was even written. The smash success of this book on publication was proof of the public's anxiety to know – a democratic right the CIA attempted to deny by immediately deleting 15–20 per cent of the original manuscript.

The questions raised in this book echo universal concern about the illegal and unethical secret operations of the CIA, and the dubious purposes to which they are often put by the government.

Never before has there been such an authoritative first-hand study of the most powerful and pervasive intelligence organisation in the world. THE CIA

'A necessary book . . . must reading for everyone'
Bestsellers

CORONET BOOKS

ISAAC ASIMOV

THE TRAGEDY OF THE MOON

In this fascinating volume one of the greatest imaginative minds in the world of science fiction turns his attention to science fact. Far from the drabness of scientific textbooks, here is a mind-bending trip into the world as it is – and as it might have been.

What would life on Earth be like if we didn't have a Moon?

Why don't we follow the clear logic of a seasonal calendar?

Must we computerize the world because we have grown too lazy to run it in any other way?

Scientist or non-scientist, layman or specialist, Asimov invites YOU to join him on a trip back into the past – and forward into the future.

CORONET BOOKS

ISAAC ASIMOV

ASIMOV ON ASTRONOMY

One of the world's foremost science fiction writers, Isaac Asimov now leaves the realms of imagination in the even more fascinating search after truth. In this remarkable book, he gives us a highly personal and entertaining insight into the history and science of astronomy, opening up amazing fields of speculation.

Could one of Earth's cities be blown to dust by a killer asteroid?

What is the true feasibility of the Moon becoming an Earth colony?

Is there a tenth planet as yet undiscovered?

Starting from Earth and its neighbours, Asimov takes us on an unforgettable trip through the solar system and the galaxies to encompass, finally, the whole universe.

CORONET BOOKS

ADRIAN BERRY

THE NEXT TEN THOUSAND YEARS

In THE NEXT TEN THOUSAND YEARS Adrian Berry puts forward his remarkable and heartening vision of man's future in the universe. Flying city states, the dismantling of Jupiter for its minerals, colonies on Venus after conversion of its atmosphere, instantaneous space journeys through 'holes' in space — these are just a few of the exciting developments predicted in this exhilarating book.

'Challenging and splendidly stimulating'   *Daily Express*

'A daring and imaginative view of how man's horizons might expand'   *Isaac Asimov*

CORONET BOOKS

MILTON SHULMAN

THE RAVENOUS EYE

Violence appears to be increasing at an alarming rate.
Contempt for politicians appears to be endemic. The
problems concerning the usage of dangerous drugs in our
society appear to become more manifold. The generation
gap between children and their parents appears to widen
too quickly. Sexual permissiveness appears to permeate
many western societies.

HOW MUCH OF THIS ACCELERATION IN BOTH FACT
AND SENSIBILITY IS DUE TO THE IMPACT OF TELE-
VISION?

'A civilised, reasonable and reasoned book. No one concerned with broadcasting should ignore it, but it will be
particularly useful to the intelligent layman in his role as
critical viewer' *The Sunday Times*

'A formidable attack' *The Observer*

'A serious and powerful case' *The Guardian*

'He argues with passion and intelligent vigour . . . a
thoughtful and stimulating book . . . a worthy one on an
important subject' *Variety*

CORONET BOOKS

ROBERT HELLER

THE COMMON MILLIONAIRE

In this witty and informative study of the millionaire class Robert Heller lays bare the truth about great wealth. The editor of *Management Today* and a well-known journalist and broadcaster, he is uniquely placed to describe those remarkable products of our age – the super-rich – and how they made their million.

'The latest in the long, winding line of "funny money" books, THE COMMON MILLIONAIRE is one of the choicest of the bunch. Fast, witty and well-informed, it has the compulsiveness of a monologue by some loquacious financial journalist full of inside news on our masters, as overheard in some City bar'   *The Times*

CORONET BOOKS

STEPHEN BARLAY

AIRCRASH DETECTIVE

Aircrash detectives track down the killers of the air — those major and minor aircraft faults which have sent hundreds to their deaths. Probing amidst the wreckage, they fight a continuous battle against time. How can they discover the killer before it strikes again?

Air disasters are a familiar headline in this age of mass jet travel. And everyone who travels by air knows that, next time, *he* may be the one to die. For only the aircrash detective's efforts can prevent a recurrence of the same terrible tragedy.

'Mr Barlay has gathered an astounding amount of material about air crashes . . . The pace is compelling, the approach responsible, and the facts beyond criticism.'
The Observer

'Mr Barlay has written an admirably thorough and timely report on air safety and he's made it exciting reading too.'
Peter Grosvenor in the *Daily Express*

CORONET BOOKS

STEPHEN BARLAY

DOUBLE CROSS

Industrial spies are the secret agents of the business world, the shadowy masters of economic espionage. They trade in valuable secrets, whether they are new formulae, revolutionary designs, secret sales figures, promotion and expansion plans, or the knowledge locked up in an executive's brain. And these frightening 'secrets' men are ruthless professionals, running world-wide industrial espionage networks.

It took Stephen Barlay seven years of manoeuvring to come face to face with these hidden men : to see the cloaks and daggers in the fashion industry ; to visit the school for spies and the factories where they produce custom-built bugging devices ; to witness the use of vast slush-funds for bribery ; to find out how to listen in on pillow-talk and boardroom-deals and how secrets are extracted from advertisements, dustbins, annual reports, typewriter ribbons and people.

Here is a book which will blow away the veils of conventional secrecy which hide the industrial spy. A documentary which reads like a thriller. DOUBLE CROSS is a horrifying exposé which will fascinate, amaze — and horrify.

CORONET BOOKS

SHIRL SOLOMON

HOW TO REALLY KNOW YOURSELF THROUGH YOUR HANDWRITING

Your handwriting can never lie.
Did you know that people reveal their true selves in their handwriting? As soon as we put pen to paper we set down an infallible personality profile for the handwriting specialist.

In this entertaining and easy-to-follow guide a hand-writing expert shows you just how to discover yourself through your handwriting. And through scrutinizing other people's writing you can find out what *they're* really like. This fascinating book offers you remarkable insights into human personality and, most interesting of all, the chance to discover the truth about yourself.

Do you look towards the future? Then your handwriting will show a desire to move ahead and the dots on your *i*'s will appear after the *i* itself. Your writing habits can reveal your tolerance, and if so you won't bother to cross out or correct a wrong letter. Or are you uncommunicative? That shows too – and rounded letters such as *a*, *o* and *d* will probably have reinforcing loops to keep them closed.

CORONET BOOKS

A. M. MAUGHAN

YOUNG PITT

'A kingdom trusted to a schoolboy's care'

From babyhood William Pitt had been trained to serve.
His father, the great Earl of Chatham, had prepared him
for a political career. No matter that the young man was
shy and retiring, for he alone could restore the family
fortunes And that was why, at the age of twenty-four,
William Pitt, a mere 'schoolboy', became Prime Minister . . .

'Miss Maughan is wonderfully persuasive . . . her novel is
absorbing. Its evocative power, its narrative urgency and
its vivid portraits . . . give it the excitement of life relived.'
The Times

'A vivid picture . . . The Young Pitt, idealistic, determined
and brilliant, is beautifully portrayed both as man and
politician, and I enjoyed this novel immensely.'
Woman's Journal
With Flair

'A generous ration of simple history . . . on this vivid background the people are painted.'
Daily Telegraph Magazine

CORONET BOOKS

ALSO AVAILABLE IN CORONET BOOKS

ANTHONY SAMPSON
☐ 21323 X The Seven Sisters   £1.00

**VICTOR MARCHETTI &
JOHN D MARKS**
☐ 20823 6 The CIA and the Cult of Intelligence £1.75

ISAAC ASIMOV
☐ 19879 6 The Tragedy of the Moon   60p
☐ 20015 4 Asimov on Astronomy   80p

ADRIAN BERRY
☐ 19924 5 The Next Ten Thousand Years   £1.00

MILTON SHULMAN
☐ 19855 9 The Ravenous Eye   75p

ROBERT HELLER
☐ 20802 3 The Common Millionaire   95p

STEPHEN BARLAY
☐ 19679 3 Sex Slavery   45p
☐ 19890 7 Aircrash Detective   95p
☐ 19952 0 Double Cross   95p

SHIRL SOLOMON
☐ 20184 3 How to Really Know Yourself
           Through Your Handwriting   75p

A. M. MAUGHAN
☐ 19951 2 Young Pitt   75p

*All these books are available at your local bookshop or newsagent, or
can be ordered direct from the publisher. Just tick the titles you want
and fill in the form below.*

Prices and availability subject to change without notice.

CORONET BOOKS, P.O. Box 11, Falmouth, Cornwall.

Please send cheque or postal order, and allow the following for
postage and packing:

U.K. — One book 19p plus 9p per copy for each additional book
ordered, up to a maximum of 73p.

B.F.P.O. and EIRE — 19p for the first book plus 9p per copy for the
next 6 books, thereafter 3p per book.

OTHER OVERSEAS CUSTOMERS — 20p for the first book and 10p
per copy for each additional book.

Name..

Address...